How I Pray

How I Pray

Edited by
JOHN WILKINS

DARTON·LONGMAN+TODD

First published in 1993 by
Darton, Longman and Todd Ltd
1 Spencer Court
140–142 Wandsworth High Street
London SW18 4JJ

ISBN 0–232–52023–2

A catalogue record for this book is available
from the British Library

Cover design: Sarah John

Phototypeset by Intype, London
Printed and bound in Great Britain
at the University Press, Cambridge

Contents

CONTENTS

Introduction

This is a book about experience. The sixteen contributors are not talking about how to pray. They are not concerned with theory. They are talking about how they actually pray.

That is a delicate thing to do – 'like undressing in public', as the Archbishop of Canterbury puts it. Prayer is part of a love affair. But just as the experience of a love affair can be described, so can the experience of prayer. In the end, the essence of a relationship always remains a secret between the people to whom it happens, and prayer is the same. But surely no reader of this book will fail to draw from it ideas about approaches and techniques that he or she can also use.

The contributors' range of religious allegiance is very wide, from Roman Catholic to evangelical, and so is their range of occupation, from civil servant to housewife, from monk to Archbishop. The seed from which this book has grown was a series of articles published in the international Catholic weekly *The Tablet*, which I edit, during Lent 1992. All these Catholic contributions are reproduced in the book, together with another eight contributions from members of other Churches, which are being published in *The Tablet* during Lent 1993.

Many of us never get far beyond the 'prayer of incompetence'. But we would like to. Perhaps we think that real prayer is only for mystics – for professionals. If this book dispels that notion, it will have fulfilled an important purpose. Some of the contributors are indeed pro-

fessionals, but others are not, and none writes in a strict-
ly professional way. They write about themselves, and
they convey something of the encounter that is open to
any man or woman who seeks to converse with the Love
who created them. It is not necessary to 'leave the world'
to achieve this, though some must do so – and even they
must love the world before they leave it. For most
people, it is through life and work in the world that this
secret must be sought. This book shows that it can be
found – for some through contemplation in action, for
some through the frame of habit, for some through the
ceremonies of the Church, for others through the Charismatic Renewal, for some through moments snatched at
the laundry, in the kitchen, at the hospital, for others
through means that hardly seem like prayer at all. Each
individual must seek a particular way. What matters is
to pray as you are. That is what this book is about.

John Wilkins
November 1992

Stalking the Spirit

Sheila Cassidy

SHEILA CASSIDY has worked for the terminally ill for many years and is now a palliative care physician in Plymouth General Hospital. She is the author of several books including Audacity to Believe *and* Good Friday People.

Prayer, said Cyril of Alexandria, is keeping company with God; it is a relationship, a dialogue between Creator and created, father and child, master and disciple and, amazingly, between lovers. How I personally relate to God depends, therefore, not only upon where I am, but upon how I am feeling. Sometimes, I suspect, it also depends upon how God is feeling.

The Christian God is a hide-and-seek God: now he is there, now he is not. You can wait for hours for him and then just when you have despaired and think he has forgotten or just not bothered to come, there he is, grinning at you.

Prayer is a waiting game; of that I have no doubt. Ann Lewin likens it to sitting on a river bank watching for a glimpse of a kingfisher:

> Prayer is like waiting for the
> Kingfisher. All you can do is
> Be where he is likely to appear, and
> Wait.

Annie Dillard, a contemporary American, talks of 'stalking the spirit': 'You have to stalk the spirit, too. You can wait forgetful anywhere, for anywhere is the way of

1

his fleet passage, and hope to catch him by the tail and shout something in his ear before he wrests away.'

'You can wait forgetful anywhere': I find that a very good description of prayer. It is a way of spending time specifically allocated to God: time given, burnt, offered as a holocaust. It is time spent neither reading nor thinking but waiting in a stance of quiet attentiveness in which self and problems are deliberately forgotten, laid aside, so that one may be available, open to God.

I like to divide prayer into two basic categories: the first is formal, or what I call 'Waste of Time Prayer'. The second category is 'Overflow Prayer': the sort of prayer that bubbles up spontaneously from somewhere deep inside during the course of the day when I am driving my car, walking by the sea, sitting at my desk, or watching television. This second type of prayer is both effortless and delightful but my experience is that it is heavily dependent upon the first. If I do not allocate specific time to prayer, if I do not have the discipline or the generosity to give time to God, this overflow of his presence into my life seems to dry up.

So, what about formal prayer? When do I do it, and what exactly do I do? In theory, of course, it does not matter at all when one prays; it can be done any time during the day, but in practice I find timing is very important. If one sees God-time as something to be fitted into the cracks of a busy schedule, the chances are that it will be squeezed out, and one will fall into bed yet again saying, 'Sorry, Lord, I'm just too tired to pray, please understand.'

Of course God understands. Alas, it is we who are deceived. The famous saying, *Laborare est orare* (To work is to pray) has been used by many a foolish Martha to justify his or her inability to be still. In the context of a life lived for God, work is indeed an on-going encounter with the Divine but it never replaces that time of exclusive loving attention which is prayer. It is not that God demands that we burn time upon his altar but that if we do not, our relationship with him will be the poorer. The workaholic husband who is too busy to spend time with his wife soon finds that their relationship has withered away. Any relationship has to be worked at if it is to survive, let alone grow and flower. Prayer is a relationship; it has to be worked at, and that is costly.

The great breakthrough for me came when I accepted that prayer was a basic necessity in my life, like eating and sleeping, and not an optional extra. From that understanding flowed the discipline to allocate a specific amount of time to God each day, in particular each morning. I find that the early morning is the most satisfactory time to pray. It is a time in which I am rarely interrupted and it has the untrodden quality of a snow-covered street before the crowds have fouled it up.

It was Fr Michael Hollings who taught me to pray in the early mornings, when he was chaplain at Oxford and I was a medical student. I used to come to the 7.40 Mass and he would be sitting huddled in his cloak praying. However early I came, it seemed, he was always there. There was a rock-like certainty about it that fascinated me, drew me to want to do the same. Eventually, I took to arriving about three-quarters of an hour before Mass: I would sit on the wall outside the chapel until he let me in and then we both sat in silence, in the dark, until it was time for Mass. This, I suppose, was my apprenticeship in waiting on God. In some ways it could not have been easier: all I had to do was get up early and sit there waiting. In other ways it was almost unbearably difficult. My mind raced or wanted to sleep. The chair was hard. My back hurt. I wriggled and fidgeted. Now, thirty years on, my mind still races or wants to go back to bed. I still wriggle and fidget and my back hurts a great deal more than it did then. So why on earth do I do it?

Before I answer that question, let me return to the actual mechanics of prayer. These days, after many years of praying little or not at all, I get up shortly after 6.15

3

in the morning. (Let me say now, quite clearly, that this early rising is always a struggle. I find there is a sort of initial inertia, like pushing a boulder off the edge of a cliff. Once I have shifted it, however, it gathers momentum.) I make a mug of tea and, clasping it to me like a comforter, sit cross-legged on the floor in my living room in front of a Rublev icon of the Trinity and a candle. I have a big hour-glass and I tip it upside down and abandon the hour to God.

This is waste-of-time prayer, holocaust time. I often feel really lousy, tired, nauseated, dreadful and long to creep back to bed, but I do not because this is God's time, not mine, and I know that its quality lies not in what I feel but in the totality of my gift. This is a time of abandonment to God, a time in which I try to still my mind and just be open, receptive to him. My prayer is totally without images and largely without words. I have no picture whatsoever of God and although I look at the icon I am not seeing the figures so much as focusing on the blur of colours and the flickering light of the candle. The icon and candle are aids in prayer and my focusing upon them is a technique to still my mind in the way that other people use a mantra or focus on their breathing. The prayer is in the act of the will, the waiting forgetful of self, the holocaust of time.

After twenty years, this emptying of the mind comes relatively easily to me, or perhaps it is more accurate to say that I am more relaxed about it than I used to be. If, as usually happens, my mind is invaded by a kaleidoscope of thoughts and ideas I simply ignore them, rather in the way women ignore their children when they are engrossed in a conversation. Some thoughts of course are too insistent to be ignored, so I gather them up and include them in my prayer. What I cannot do is shut thoughts out altogether. Annie Dillard likens this effort to be still to trying to gag the commentator at a ball game, or damming a river in spate:

4

The world's spiritual geniuses seem to discover that the mind's muddy river, this ceaseless flow of trivia and trash, cannot be dammed, and that trying to dam it is a waste of effort that might lead to madness. Instead you must allow the muddy river to flow unheeded in the dim channels of consciousness; you raise your sights: you look along it, mildly, acknowledging its presence without interest and gazing beyond it into the realm of the real where subjects and objects act and rest purely without utterance.

Among the flotsam and jetsam that flow along this river of the mind I find fragments of Scripture and psalms. These rise up in an automatic fashion, the way a phrase from a song will go round and round in one's head. These fragments I take as mantras which have been given, and use them for my prayer in a way that is barely conscious. I may find myself repeating, for example, 'Holy God, holy and strong, holy and deathless, have mercy on us,' or, 'Create a clean heart for me, O God.'

These automatic spoken prayers will often fade away into a much deeper quiet in which I simply rest, empty, before God. It is my experience that this use of what is 'given' is quite different from deliberately choosing a phrase of my own which seems somehow to get in the way of stillness.

Abbot John Chapman, a monk of Downside and a great spiritual director, is famous for his advice, 'Pray as you can, not as you can't.' If I can sit silent and empty before God, like a beggar with his bowl waiting to be filled, then that is how I do it. Sometimes, however, I am too tired or too restless to be still, and take up a prayer book or switch on some music. I have returned quite recently to the use of the breviary and find great solace in the psalms. I am constantly amazed at the richness of the Divine Office. I love the hymns especially for their poetry and their pure theology:

Transcendent God in whom we live.
The resurrection and the light . . .

Eternal ever-living God
who made us from the dust of earth,
Transform us by the Spirit's grace
Give value to our little worth.

I have come of recent years to value the formal words of liturgy more than my own words. While I find it quite easy to write prayers for other people, I do not use words of that kind in my own prayer. The psalms and hymns seem to work as a sort of magic carpet carrying me to God when my wordless imageless chariot fails. Most of the time I use the same translation of the psalms (Gelineau). Their familiarity is comforting and I know a few of them by heart. (I find a particular delight in walking on the beach reciting psalms 138, 62 or 91.) Sometimes, however, I try a different translation; my favourite is the reworking of the psalms by Jim Cotter.

The psalms seem to articulate my longing better than any words I can find for myself, so that I only use my own words at times when I am in total despair over lost keys or a car that will not start – or so besotted that all I can do is mutter, I love you, I love you, I love you.

I suppose the way individuals pray depends a great deal upon their God-concept, upon which of God's many faces they relate to. I have very little sense of God as Father or Mother, probably to do with my own experience of parenting, but a powerful sense of God as Creator, as Master and sometimes as Lover. I live quite comfortably with the paradox of God as transcendent and therefore unknowable and God as personal and closer than the neck of my camel. My eyes fix on the winter sun and my heart yearns for the divine wisdom, that 'breath of the power of God, pure emanation of the glory of the Almighty', the 'reflection of the eternal Light, untarnished mirror of God's active power' (Wisd. 7:26).

This sense of the transcendence and unknowability of God does not, however, seem to impede me from telling him how awful I feel in the morning or from asking him, frantically, to start my car in the rain. Since I pray out of my own need, not out of God's, I feel no necessity to tell him what needs doing. I lay the broken world at his feet in total confidence that he knows what he is about, and yet, quite illogically, I pray with enormous urgency for him to create for me a clean heart and put a new spirit within me.

The prayer I have described is what goes on for me between 6.30 and 7.30 each morning and for ten minutes before I go to bed. When that is done, I try to read a little. I have always had more difficulty timetabling Scripture and spiritual reading into my life than actual prayer. At the moment I try to spend 20 minutes or so sitting on my bed in my room which overlooks the sea and reading. I have just finished Gerry Hughes's *God of Surprises* for the second time and am tempted to return instantly to chapter one for, as the years go by, I find myself drawn more and more to Ignatian spirituality. At first it was the Ignatian ideal of a life of action flowing from contemplation which appealed to me but I am now beginning to face the possibility that there is something of value in imaginative prayer.

Let me explain. Most of my life I have prayed the way I have just described: without words and without images, spurning all suggestions that I should try to picture the gospel scenes and see what they said to me. That sort of prayer I reckoned was OK for other people but it just was not my thing. On a recent retreat, however, it was suggested that as a way into imaginative prayer I might like to draw. As a natural doodler, I took to this like a duck to water and was amazed at how my childish illustration of the Gospel spoke to me. Images flowed from my pen in much the same way that words do and reflected back to me more than I would have thought possible. Illustrating Peter's betrayal of Jesus, I drew a

7

dejected Peter sitting on a bench outside Pilate's court – and then, quite unbidden, a Jesus in chains appeared to comfort him. I know the Gospel does not tell the story like that, but my drawing revealed to me something of the forgiveness of God that I had not known before. For me, I suppose, the drawing is another route into my unconscious and into my relationship with God.

This experience with exploring the gospels is having all sorts of knock-on effects. I have long considered myself theocentric rather than christocentric and have always loved the Old Testament in preference to the New, enchanted by the poetry and amazing imagery of Isaiah, Job, Wisdom and the like. Now, rather late in the day, I find myself drawn also to the gospels, to wonder about Jesus the man and his times and places. A recent brief study of the Apostolic Fathers has opened new doors for me, catching glimpses of larger-than-life figures like Ignatius of Antioch who walked in chains from Antioch to Rome to be united with his lover God in the arena.

How strange it is to hold in tension the crazy words of such martyrs, 'Let me be ground to become the pure wheat of Christ,' and the daily tedium of prayer. What has my dragging myself untimely from my bed each morning to do with Ignatius' wild protestations of love? Amazingly, I know it has everything to do with it. Daily fidelity to prayer has brought me to a place where I know such claims to be true. 'Walk the dark ways of faith', says Augustine, 'and you will attain the vision of God.'

I find it difficult to explain the paradox that prayer can be hard, arid, dry and yet also marvellous. It is not just that the fleeting glory of the kingfisher catches one by surprise, but that even in the lonely desert of a Plymouth morning God is present. It is not that God manifests himself by lights or visions or music, nor even in consolation (though consolation there often is), it is just a dark knowledge that this is time well spent, that the holocaust has been received.

Easier to explain is the overflow into the rest of life,

the prayer that erupts unbidden in moments of stillness, of joy or of difficulty. There is the power, too, the strength given for service which seems always renewed, although it never relieves one of vulnerability or foolishness. How well I understand, these days, about earthen vessels, about strength which is at its best in weakness.

More than anything, though, I am conscious of the joy. In his 'Winged Horse', Hilaire Belloc writes:

> For you that took the all-in-all the things you
>   left were three.
> A loud voice for singing and keen eyes to
>   see,
> And a spouting well of joy within that never
>   yet was dried!
> And I ride.

This laughing well of joy I see as the spring of living water of which Jesus spoke when addressing the Samaritan woman in John 4:10: 'If you only knew what God is offering you,' he said. 'The water that I shall give will turn into a spring inside you, welling up to eternal life.'

Now that I have tasted this water I know the truth of the line in psalm 62: 'your love is better than life itself.'

The last word must go to Meister Eckhart (if indeed it was he who said it):

> Put on your jumping shoes
> And jump into the heart of God.

In Jesus' Name

Bede Griffiths

BEDE GRIFFITHS is a Benedictine monk, born in England and educated at Christ's Hospital and Oxford. After twenty years as a monk in England he went to India 'to find the other half of his soul'. At Shantivanam, the Christian ashram he leads in Tamil Nadu, his prophetic witness has created a world centre of spiritual unity.

If anyone asks me how I pray, my simple answer is that I pray the Jesus prayer. Anyone familiar with the story of a Russian pilgrim will know what I mean. It consists simply in repeating the words: 'Lord Jesus Christ, Son of God, have mercy on me, a sinner.' I have used this prayer now for over forty years and it has become so familiar that it simply repeats itself. Whenever I am not otherwise occupied or thinking of something else, the prayer goes quietly on. Sometimes it is almost mechanical, just quietly repeating itself, and other times it gathers strength and can become extremely powerful.

I give it my own interpretation. When I say, 'Lord Jesus Christ, Son of God,' I think of Jesus as the Word of God, embracing heaven and earth and revealing himself in different ways and under different names and forms to all humanity. I consider that this Word 'enlightens everyone coming into the world', and though they may not recognize it, it is present to every human being in the depths of their soul. Beyond word and thought, beyond all signs and symbols, this Word is being secretly spoken in every heart in every place and

10

at every time. People may be utterly ignorant of it or may choose to ignore it, but whenever or wherever anyone responds to truth or love or kindness, to the demand for justice, concern for others, care of those in need, they are responding to the voice of the Word. So also when anyone seeks truth or beauty in science, philosophy, poetry or art, they are responding to the inspiration of the Word.

I believe that that Word took flesh in Jesus of Nazareth and in him we can find a personal form of the Word to whom we can pray and to whom we can relate in terms of love and intimacy, but I think that he makes himself known to others under different names and forms. What counts is not so much the name and the form as the response in the heart to the hidden mystery, which is present to each one of us in one way or another and awaits our response in faith and hope and love.

When I say 'Have mercy on me, a sinner', I unite myself with all human beings from the beginning of the world, who have experienced separation from God, or from the eternal truth. I realize that, as human beings, we are all separated from God, from the source of our being. We are wandering in a world of shadows, mistaking the outward appearance of people and things for reality. But at all times something is pressing us to reach out beyond the shadows, to face the reality, the truth, the inner meaning of our lives, and so to find God, or whatever name we give to the mystery which enfolds us.

So I say the Jesus prayer, asking to be set free from the illusions of this world, from the innumerable vanities and deceits with which I am surrounded. And I find in the name of Jesus the name which opens my heart and mind to reality. I believe that each one of us has an inner light, an inner guide, which will lead us through the shadows and illusions by which we are surrounded, and open our minds to the truth. It may come through poetry or art, or philosophy or science, or more commonly through the encounter with people and events, day by day. Personally I find that meditation, morning and evening, every day, is the best and most direct method of getting in touch with reality. In meditation I try to let go of everything of the outer world of the senses, of the inner world of thoughts, and listen to the inner voice, the voice of the Word, which comes in the silence, in the stillness when all activity of mind and body ceases. Then in the silence I become aware of the presence of God, and I try to keep that awareness during the day. In bus or train or travelling by air, in work or study or talking and relating to others, I try to be aware of this presence in everyone and in everything. And the Jesus prayer is what keeps me aware of the presence.

So prayer for me is the practice of the presence of God in all situations, in the midst of noise and distractions of all sorts, of pain and suffering and death, as in times of peace and quiet, of joy and friendship, of prayer and silence, the presence is always there. For me the Jesus prayer is just a way of keeping in the presence of God.

I find it convenient to keep in mind the four stages of prayer in the medieval tradition – *lectio*, *meditatio*, *oratio*, *contemplatio*.

Lectio is reading. Most people need to prepare themselves for prayer by reading of some sort. Reading the Bible is the traditional way, but this reading is not just reading for information. It is an attentive reading, savouring the words as in reading poetry. For this reason I prefer the authorized or revised versions of the Bible, which preserve the rich, poetic tradition of the English language.

Lectio is followed by *meditatio*. This means reflecting on one's reading, drawing out the deeper sense and preserving it in the 'heart'. It is said that Mary 'pondered all these things in her heart'. This is meditation in the traditional sense, bringing out the moral and symbolic meaning of the text and applying it to one's own life. The symbolic meaning goes beyond the literal, and shows all its implications for one's own life and for the life of the Church and the world. It is a great loss when the literal meaning, of which today, of course, we have a far greater knowledge, leaves no place for the deeper, richer symbolic meaning which points to the ultimate truth to which the Scripture bears witness.

Meditation is naturally followed by prayer – *oratio*. Our understanding of the deeper meaning of the text depends on our spiritual insight, and this comes from prayer. Prayer is opening the heart and mind to God, that is, it is going beyond all the limited processes of the rational mind and opening the mind to the transcendent reality to which all words and thoughts are pointing. This demands devotion – that is, self-surrender. As long as we remain on the level of the rational mind, we are governed by our ego, our independent, rational self. We can make use of all kinds of assistance, of commentaries and spiritual guides, but as long as the individual self remains in command, we are imprisoned in the rational mind with its concepts and judgements. Only when we surrender the ego, the separate self, and turn to God, the supreme Spirit, can we receive the light which we need to understand the deeper meaning of the Scriptures. This is passing from *ratio* to *intellectus*, from discursive thought to intuitive insight.

So we pass to *contemplatio*. Contemplation is the goal of all Christian life. It is knowledge by love. St Paul often prays for his disciples that they may have knowledge (*gnosis*) and understanding (*epignosis*) in the mystery of Christ. The mystery of Christ is the ultimate truth, the reality towards which all human life aspires. And this mystery is known by love. Love is going out of oneself, surrendering the self, letting the reality, the truth take over. It is not limited to any earthly object or person. It reaches out to the infinite and the eternal. This is contemplation. It is not something which we achieve for ourselves. It is something that comes when we let go. We have to abandon everything – all words, thoughts,

13

hopes, fears, all attachments to ourselves or to any earthly thing, and let the divine mystery take possession of our lives. It feels like death and is a sort of dying. It is encountering the darkness, the abyss, the void. It is facing nothingness – or as the English Benedictine mystic Augustine Baker said, it is the 'union of the nothing with the Nothing'.

This is the negative aspect of contemplation. The positive aspect is, of course, the opposite. It is total fulfilment, total wisdom, total bliss, the answer to all problems, the peace which surpasses understanding, the joy which is the fullness of love. St Paul has summed it up in the letter to the Ephesians – or whoever wrote that letter which is the supreme example of Christian *gnosis*:

I bow my knees before the Father, from whom every family in heaven and on earth is named, that according to the riches of his glory, he may strengthen you with his spirit in the inner man; that Christ may dwell in your hearts by faith, that being rooted and grounded in love, you may have power to comprehend with all the saints what is the length and breadth and height and depth, and may know the love of Christ which surpasses knowledge, that you may be filled with all the fullness of God. (Eph. 3:14–19)

Conversation with God

George Carey

GEORGE CAREY is Archbishop of Canterbury and former Bishop of Bath and Wells. He is the author of several books including The Great God Robbery *and* I Believe.

Disclosing how one prays is a little like undressing in public – more of you is revealed than you would like and you are not sure if others will appreciate it. I suppose that another reticence I had when invited to contribute to this series is that I know only too well how much I still have to discover about prayer. Archbishops too have so much to learn about God and his ways with human beings.

So, if I am going to tell you about my kind of praying you will need to know something about my pilgrimage – because pilgrimage and prayer are very much one.

Prayer started for me when my Christian journey began. I began going to church in my late teens. I had emerged from the war years a troubled young man asking questions like: 'Can there be a God if such awful things happen to good people?' And yet, I wondered as I saw the way that so many people behaved: how can there not be a God when I see so much goodness, bravery, beauty, joy and goodness in ordinary people?

My brother Bob introduced me to the local Anglican church where he had been attending the Sunday School. God suddenly became real. Indeed, I could identify with the story of Paul Claudel who, after his conversion, leaned against a pillar in Notre Dame cathedral and is said to have exclaimed: 'O God, suddenly you have become for me a person!' So, prayer flowed from this new relationship: God was someone with whom I could talk. To this day that is the case. If prayer presupposes a relationship, then every minute of the day is a conversation with God. I talk with him silently in the middle of a business meeting, as I walk along a road and when I am walking my dog in the garden. When I am alone I speak aloud to him; I meditate aloud, I voice my frustrations and pour out my thanksgiving. I learned from the Psalms long ago that prayer is not like learning a foreign language but is an honest relationship with someone who loves us deeply and whom we love in return.

Somewhere along the way I learned to relate Scripture and prayer. Perhaps that came naturally out of the evangelical tradition which I inherited. If so, I am endlessly grateful for this insight, because prayer is enriched by a scriptural base. I usually read four chapters every day, following a lectionary first used by the Scottish divine Robert Murray McCheyne. The course of readings takes me through the whole Bible once a year and the Psalms and New Testament twice. One of those chapters I study at a deeper level, using the Greek text. I find that prayer arises naturally from that source as I meditate slowly and reflectively on the passages.

How do I meditate on Scripture? Let me give you an example. Take Ephesians 1:3: 'Blessed be the God and Father of our Lord Jesus Christ, who has blessed us in Christ with every spiritual blessing in the heavenly places.' I might well start with reflecting upon the link between 'God' and 'Father'; between a God who confronts us all as a mysterious Creator and a God who is for us as 'Father'. What does it mean? What about those who cannot call God, Father? How might this relationship affect my life today? . . . and so on. Meditation on Scripture is doing theology – and doing theology is prayer. For me, there can be no separation of academic theological interests from spirituality. Didymus the Blind said: 'To theologise is to praise.' We must learn to pray with our minds as well as our hearts. Adoration is the lifting of the mind to God.

Returning to the passage from Ephesians, my meditation might take me on to consider other key words in the text – 'he has *blessed us* in Christ'. What does this mean? I might try to make sense of it in terms of the Church's story or my own experience. I might well seek to see it in the context of those for whom God is absent. How does one bring together my experience of 'blessing' and another's experience of darkness and death? What difference might this meditation have on my life today when I come into contact with people for whom God is just a three-letter word?

When I am in residence at Lambeth my daily programme usually starts at 6.00 a.m. After a quick shower my dog, Buccleuch, and I walk briskly in the garden. Then I go into my study for prayer and reflection on the text of Scripture. By this time it will be around 7.00 a.m. and there is a slight pause as I make tea for myself and Eileen, my wife, before we join the Lambeth community in chapel for morning worship.

Before the service I go alone into the chapel for a further period of quiet prayer and reflection. The visit to Taizé last year with a thousand young Anglicans reminded me of my need to be still. While I was there I felt God say to me: 'You are such an activist. You have got to learn to be still – so start the day by being quiet!' I am still not very good at it.

When I was a young Christian I was taught that the four major elements of prayer are: adoration, confession, thanksgiving and supplication – making a neat mnemonic, ACTS. It was very useful to me at the time but I have to say that these days it is all a huge jumble; I do not any longer group my prayers in such a tidy package. However, there are two elements which stand out.

First, I regard praise and thanksgiving as crucial since they focus greatly on the character of God. Praise has to

17

do with who God is and what he has done. As I begin with praise so I recall my smallness and God's greatness and strength. Praise reminds us that in spite of ourselves God will always have the last word and will do his work in spite of what the Church gets up to. Praise, like the focus on a camera, gets everything in the picture into perspective. Yes, it is possible even to thank God for that wretched meeting you have to attend today, because God is never absent from any part of life. Augustine is supposed to have said: 'He who praises prays twice.'

A second element is petition. Our Lord answers prayer. If prayer is to do with a relationship, then it stands to reason that God will hear our requests and will respond. But let me add that I leave the answer to him to do as he wills. As a God of love he can be trusted with all the things I worry about – sickness, pain, the future, even death itself. So petition has its place along-side other elements in prayer. Because God is, we can pray in confidence.

But to return to my daily pattern: at 7.40 a.m. our community worship begins with a number of Lambeth residents together in my beautiful and ancient chapel. In addition to the morning Office, the sacrament of Holy Communion is celebrated three times a week. Deeply meaningful for me is the sacramental reality that there within the forms of bread and wine Our Lord deigns to make himself known. In Anglican fashion I remain agnostic about the way he chooses. However, I have no doubt that he is present for me and all those who love his appearing. Prayer then focuses on this 'timeless moment' when the stupendous events of Calvary and the passing moments of history become one. Christ is present and joy is experienced.

I resist very firmly the idea that valid prayer is only that praying which we do alone. Corporate worship is also prayer. I treasure very highly the rich language of my tradition. Repetition has helped me to store up wonderful prayers which I can recite when I am away from books. Collects like:

> Lord of All Power and Might
> The author and giver of all good things,
> Graft in our hearts the love of thy name,
> increase in us true religion.
> Nourish us in all goodness
> and of thy great mercy keep us in the same,
> Through Jesus Christ Our Lord.

Although I am among those who want to see the liturgy in a form which is accessible to all, I am convinced that too much liturgical change actually disturbs the storing up of rich prayers in the hearts and minds of the young and, indeed, of us all. The repetition of good prayers, rich in theology and resonant with beautiful images, deepens prayer and aids devotion. Although I can pray anywhere, I do find that focusing my attention on, say, candles, a simple icon or a relevant picture draws my attention and assists my prayer.

Similarly, the language of hymns and spiritual songs is so helpful. I think we often fail to appreciate this element of worship. Many of them are very wonderful prayers in their own right and, not infrequently, when words fail or when I cannot concentrate, I take a hymnal and go to a section that is relevant to my thinking. Hymns are not as a rule great poetry viewed from the intellectual point of view but they can touch the heart – and the heart is an important factor in prayer. Here are two verses from 'Morning Glory', one of my favourite hymns, written by Canon William Vanstone. The hymn speaks of the gift of Christ. Incidentally, this is one hymn that is very good poetry:

> Open are the gifts of God,
> gifts of love to mind and sense;
> hidden is love's agony,
> love's endeavour, love's expense.

> Therefore he who shows us God
> helpless hangs upon the tree;
> and the nails and crown of thorns
> tell of what God's love must be.

Let me make it clear, however, that prayer does not end when I leave my chapel. As prayer flows from a relationship, it flows into every area of life. I relate it to my reading – whether theology or politics or whatever. As I have already mentioned, I take a deep enjoyment in reading theology, and being stretched mentally is, for me, a form of praying. I have just finished Jurgen Moltmann's *The Spirit of Life* and volume four of Von Balthasar's *Glory of the Lord*. Both these books are seminal writings which have enabled me to glimpse new insights about God and my spiritual journey. Without doubt, reading such books is for me a form of praying.

And so thirty-five years after I started to pray, what have I gained from it all? Does it simply reveal that I am a slightly mystical, religious animal? Actually I never see myself in that light. There have been moments of deep darkness in my pilgrimage, feeling at times that God is absent. There have been many moments of rebellion, when I have not wanted to pray and when I have invented a thousand excuses to avoid meeting God in the silence – often successfully, I fear.

But I am glad to say that, through the exercise of this spiritual muscle, prayer has become easier over the years. There are many times now when I simply long to be quiet in God's presence, but the busyness of my ministry does not often allow me to be there. I console myself on those occasions that, as my theology of prayer stems from a relationship that will never end, so my prayer life will go on deepening and developing until I will one day see him face to face.

Yes, prayer is mysterious but, as George Herbert put it so beautifully, when we pray something is understood:

Prayer the Church's banquet, Angel's age,
God's breath in man returning to his birth,
The soul in paradise, heart in pilgrimage,
The Christian plummet sounding heav'n and earth:

Engine against th'Almighty, sinners' tower,
Reversed thunder, Christ-side-piercing spear,
The six days world transposing in an hour,
A kind of tune, which all things hear and fear;

Softness and peace and joy, and love, and bliss,
Exalted Manna, gladness of the best,
Heaven in ordinary, man well drest,
The milky way, the bird of paradise,

Church-bells beyond the stars heard, the soul's blood,
The land of spices; something understood.

A Woman's Discipleship

Margaret Hebblethwaite

MARGARET HEBBLETHWAITE has been involved since 1982 in giving the Ignatian Spiritual Exercises in daily life. Her books include Motherhood and God, Finding God in All Things, Basic is Beautiful, *and a book for children about prayer called* My Secret Life.

The first thing I have to admit when asked how I pray, is that I am not good at it. Although I have learnt (over the years of dabbling in Ignatian spirituality) some tools of prayer, and several ways of responding to various difficulties that come up, the fact remains that I am not as faithful and regular about my praying as I ought to be. I know that I need to listen myself to some of the advice I give to others, who come to me for spiritual direction.

I often say, for example, that a lot of the effort is taken out of praying if one can find the right time of day and the right place: then prayer becomes part of the regular rhythm of life instead of a decision that has to be made afresh for each day. I have never really found that right time of day, and even a six-month-long retreat that I made recently – which forced me to find a half-hour prayer period in virtually every day – totally failed to leave me with a 'right time of day' that fitted and stuck when the retreat came to an end.

Place, however, I find easier than time. Ideally it would be nice to have a prayer room, but that is a luxury few can afford, especially when there are five in the family.

Instead I made a little cubby-hole under the stairs into a 'prayer hole' over ten years ago, and that continues to be the place I most frequently use. It is too tiny to stand up in and has no window – only a grating to the outside air – but it is not damp and many have prayed in worse conditions. Lit by candles it has quite an atmosphere, and I can leave up whatever pictures I find helpful. I have a poignantly tender face of Christ by Leonardo – from an art calendar I bought in Siena cathedral. And I have a photograph of a clay sculpture by the Indian-influenced Catholic artist, Caroline Mackenzie, in which the pregnant body of the Mother turns into a big pot. I think of it less as Mary than as an image of the maternal dignity of God – all round and full and ripe and capacious. I also have a few objects with special meaning to me from around the world: a clump of sheep's wool picked off the hills behind St Beuno's on my 'resurrection day' in an eight-day retreat; a lump of reddish stone from a mine in Bilbao, that says something to me about labour and labourers; a small metal crucifix, that my youngest son's godmother held up in fear and hope in a sur-rounded Polish factory, as she addressed the troops through a megaphone held in the other hand; and a wooden pendant of a woman releasing a dove, which was given me by the Committee of Mothers of Heroes and Martyrs in Nicaragua – very much the symbol of the liberated woman and her call to sacrifice, courage and perseverance.

Most important of all, perhaps, is my prayer stool: I could not find any shops that sold these useful little benches – except for a posh Church of England outfit in Westminster that could provide a polished, upholstered little number for some fantastic price – so I wrote in desperation to a Carmelite convent where I had heard all the nuns used them. They sent me one in a parcel by return of post, and I felt as soon as I perched on it that it had been well prayed on before me. This prayer

23

stool enables me to keep a position that is both comfortable and reverent, a position that I use only for prayer.

Another way in which I am not 'good at prayer' is that when I pray there seems so much trash to clear out of the way from my everyday preoccupations. My prime concerns well up and think themselves out and slowly are laid before the feet of God – and it takes such a while that there is little time left for anything else. Yet if I have brought my anxieties and preoccupations before God and looked at them in the conscious awareness of God's presence, and come eventually to some provisional peace about them with God, then my prayer has been worthwhile. I sometimes picture myself as a disturbed pool where slowly the ripples fade away until the water is still and the depths of the pool come into view.

Assume, now, that I have found time and place, that I have settled myself upon my prayer stool and that I have cleared away the top level of trash. What then? Scripture is nearly always the key to my prayer, by which I really mean the gospels, for that is where I find Jesus. And as I read, I know exactly who I am in the story. In John 1 we read about two disciples of John the Baptist. I think they had come to an end of what they could learn from John, but felt quite unable to return to their former lives. And so, when John pointed at Jesus, they started to walk after him. He turned and said, 'What are you looking for?' And they said (neither answering nor avoiding the question), 'Where do you live?' One of them was Andrew, the other was unnamed. That one is me. I am neither male nor female (if I were female I would be excluded from the inner twelve, and if I were male I would not be myself). In every gospel story, I am there as the same disciple, hanging on, remembering much, doing little, more observing than observed.

Often in my prayer, I do not open my Bible, but go straight to one of my favourite spots – the upper room. The more alienated I feel from the sexism of the Mass as currently practised in our churches, with a men-only line-up at the altar, the more readily I climb in my imagination the wooden stairs to the upper room, and knock on the door, and find Jesus opening to me and asking me in. Sometimes I am the first to arrive but more often the room is full of people – the dead as well as the living, those dear to me as well as those I know only from repute. And I am welcomed among them to share this time of refreshment. Sometimes I am so troubled and worn that Jesus simply invites me to come into an inner room where I can sleep in peace. At other times Jesus comes to me when I sit down and he washes my feet, and as he does I tell him why I am unworthy and he washes it all away.

But most often we all sit round the table and he passes around the crumbly brown bread of his body and the rich red wine of his life blood. I watch as it passes from hand to hand, passing to the martyrs of El Salvador, or to the original apostles, or to my friends or relatives, or to others whose love of God has touched me in one way or another, until it reaches me. And I leave the upper room refreshed for the work ahead, for there is nothing in that Last Supper of my imagination that hurts or offends me as a woman. (Nor indeed was there anything offensive in the Last Supper of history, where, as Carla Ricci has shown, women were almost undoubtedly present: the failure to record their presence is no reason at all to assume their absence, as we can see from comparing other gospel texts – 'those who ate the loaves were five thousand men' (Mark 6:44) and (Matt. 14:21) 'those who ate were about five thousand men, besides women and children'.)

Of course, as well as times set aside just for prayer, there are also times when we pray while doing something else – when we are travelling, for example, or ironing, or having a shower. Since taking a job at *The Tablet*, which involves me in driving regularly from Oxford to London, I have begun to listen to Scripture on the road. I have bought the entire New Testament on cassettes (it is quite reasonably priced in an old Authorized Version recording) and I always keep one tape in the car with me. If sitting in a traffic jam is frustrating, it is a bonus to have some time to listen to the words of Jesus – the sweetest words I know, and yet the most challenging ones too. In theory I can hear the whole of each gospel through on a few journeys; in practice I am rarely able to take in more than two or three stories before my mind begins to blank out. At that point – or preferably before – it is time to turn off the tape and hold on for a few moments to whatever was welling up from what I have heard, letting the light of Scripture shine like a lamp on the page of my life.

Concentration, however, is difficult while driving. Sometimes I am too tired after a long day's work to take in any words at all, and I opt for the soothing effects of music, that lets my thoughts scatter hither and thither without the discipline of thinking on determined lines. This is, I believe, another form of pool-settling and a process that I cannot skip. It is as though my mind needs to run riot if it is to tidy up and file away my thoughts – rather as in sleep. And yet when my tired mind goes wild like this, I am not unable to pray, but rather enabled to pray in a different way, not putting one thought after another, let alone stringing together words, but seeking to find softness and warmth and acceptance in letting go to God.

But my most satisfying prayer has certainly been in my rare periods of retreat. Instead of starting again from scratch each time I pray – stilling myself, letting God enter the overriding concerns of my life, and finally only just beginning to be receptive at a deeper level – all this can be done once and for all if I have the opportunity to stay in a spirit of silence, undisturbed for a few days, freed from the need to respond to others or to produce work or to sort out problems or even to talk. It has been in the times of retreat that the most blessed moments have occurred – combining a shame-filled gratitude with a rapturous self-gift – and these moments stand as a beacon not only to my ordinary prayer but also to every day of my life. As in marriage, once I am given, it is for life.

'Humming' and Patient Attentiveness

Jim Cotter

JIM COTTER has ministered in parishes and theological education in the Church of England. He writes books which seek to reshape the prayer of the Christian inheritance and make connections between faith and everyday life. At his home in Sheffield he offers hospitality for prayer and reflection in the city.

How *do* I pray? A daunting question. Much easier to write about prayer, somewhat easier to compile prayers. Very tempting to claim more than is in practice true, to say that I pray for longer periods of time than I do, or more frequently, or better. I am haunted by that old directive that the heart of the work of the ordained minister is to pray and to teach others to pray. And so I am aware of the danger of pride – and even of exaggerated penitence! I think too of an Indian doctor who once said to me, 'Beware of the three Ps – physicians, priests, politicians. All are con men. Sometimes their games are worth playing for a while, but don't take any of them too seriously.'

So I shall attempt some truth-telling, and that in itself may be a prayer that cleanses and invigorates.

At my home in Sheffield I try to provide hospitality for prayer and reflection in the city. I find myself saying that I am trying to provide 'nothing' as well as I can – to create an atmosphere and a space that is uncluttered and quiet. And from time to time I seek to do that for myself. It is a process of becoming quiet, of stilling a physical or mental restlessness. I may begin by sitting still or by walking slowly and gently, in tune with my breathing and in time with a 'hum', repeating a phrase to distract distractions. The impish part of me (originating I suspect from the day I hiccoughed through my baptism in a Methodist church on what was then called Temperance Sunday) is pleased with the word 'hum'. Why call it a 'mantra' when the homely English tradition has a perfectly good word popularized by a fictional character dear to the heart of the childlike? I do have to admit, though, that the words I use are Greek – in fact the Jesus Prayer in the words, 'Kyrie Jesu Christe Huios Theos Eleison'.

Well, I have hummed my way along a beach at Exmouth early on summer mornings before a day's work preparing some talks on sexuality and spirituality. I have hummed those ancient words around the edge of a playing field in Sheffield – and in many other occasional places. (The only caution is that I should walk where I do not have to look where I am putting my feet.)

So that is one way in which I begin to pray – fitfully and irregularly. Something is missing when I neglect it for too long. My 'godfriend' once referred to it as 'plonk' prayer: you just place yourself in the presence of the Great Mystery we call God, expectant but without any expectations, and try to do precisely nothing. It is as humdrum as the 'plonk' from the supermarket shelves. In terms of a provable link with useful results, there is nothing to show. And yet . . . the truly creative and prayerful may happen only when I give space and time to *nothing*. The hardest thing to do is to protect the boundaries of such time and space, to give this emptiness priority. Who was it who said that we do what is urgent, not what is important?

It is all suspiciously akin to writing this chapter. I had to allow myself time simply to hold the theme in my mind and heart and not do anything. Then I had to set aside the time to write, to sit down and to get going. That is much more difficult than the actual writing. Would I be writing it now if there was not the pressure of a 'deadline'? And is it the Creator Spirit who is pressing gently but insistently, soul-deep within me, saying that the 'lines' will go 'dead' if I do not respond?

Sometimes nothing at all happens in the time of nothing. It becomes a time of waiting, even of endurance, a time of watching and listening with the still, patient attentiveness of the birdwatcher. But once in a while something does happen. As a wordsmith I find it is words that begin to be given, even to flow, surfacing intermittently like a stream in limestone country, always to my surprise. Then I find I need to give loving and accurate attention to whatever it is that is emerging, and to test it against what I have already learned of the ways of God. That in turn may lead to a passionate engagement with words and ideas, shaping them according to whatever talent I have, sifting them through my perceptions of truth, aware of how easily distortions and partiality creep in.

Am I now talking about praying or about writing? Or is there really little difference between the two? I certainly find myself responding to the rhythms of quieting and scribbling, of waiting and shaping, of contemplative attending and active participation, perhaps of praying and living. Maybe the very best praying that I do is in and through this very process of writing. Dare I claim to be participating in a small way in the creative loving of God, putting in my pennyworth to the golden guinea of the divine gift? If so, then the writing is to be thought of not as akin to the praying but as a sample of the praying. Not, 'My prayer is like this,' but, 'Here is a way in which my praying is actually done.'

I also realize that such gifts 'happen' in a conversation between two 'friends in God' as they seek to discern patterns and meaning and directions in the life of one or other of them. In the loving and accurate attention given to what really matters in human life, I do find myself from time to time thinking and saying what I have never before thought or said. And it is often a gift as much to myself as to the one whose story I am listening to. In focusing on the particularities of *this* moment, *this* person, *these* circumstances, in having the courage to face what is going on, and in being open to the Other who may be expected both to welcome and to challenge, that which is new is given. The moment of surprise and insight may provoke gratitude or penitence or a gentle thoughtfulness. 'I'm loved *that* much.' 'I didn't realize the harm I was causing.' 'Now I *see*.' My praying deepens in the realizing, and I do well to expand my awareness of the gift, to relish it, to chew on it. Again, the praying and the living are becoming one.

There is something I find important here about my praying for others. If I can keep alive within me this being expectant of the unexpected, if I experience – both in solitude and in conversation – the gift of that which is new, then there may be a Spirit at work within us and among us that is mostly hidden and which cannot be measured or grasped, but which is having a profound influence upon us. It is into that possibility that I place the names of the ones for whom I have a concern. The word I use is the simple 'Bless . . .' Nothing more specific. After all, there is nothing more I would wish than that others receive a measure of that abundant life implied by a 'blessing'. And it may be that the fitful, almost perfunctory mention of a name triggers a movement of the Spirit. The cosmic net trembles, vibrating with the whispers of prayer. Why should geography or death impede that communication?

In the background to these ways of praying is the Great Story – of God, of Christ, of the People of God. Again I try to bring heart and mind and body to the point of loving attention and passionate engagement as I place my short story in the context of the long epic. So

I am drawn to participating in the Eucharist, once or twice a week, listening to that day's extracts from the Story and sharing in the re-enactment and re-membering of the central drama. I find that the prayer is often a struggle because we continue to 'do this' together in ways that speak too much of coercive power, of kings and judges in imperial courts who need to be placated and to be pleaded with for mercy. It is a painfully prayerful task to keep loyal to the God of deeper and more wide-ranging love.

If I am to learn and to take to my whole being 'the mind of Christ' – the character of Christ becoming my character – then I need to hear other accents in the Story, to cherish and absorb the parts of Scripture that give me clues about God the persistent Lover and Friend, God the nurturing Mother, God the Wise Healer. I find it a discipline of prayer to ask into what image and likeness of God I am intended to grow. Help comes to me through poetry and art, music and sculpture – and in the writings of the theologians of our own day who struggle to make the ways of God clear to us. My praying is 'informed' and fed by such people as John V. Taylor, Rosemary Haughton, W.H. Vanstone, Alan Ecclestone and Neville Ward.

By compiling books of prayers, using psalms and scripture readings and canticles, but being alert also to the history of faith since the first century and to the images and experiences of the twentieth, I have been asking, What in all that we have inherited do I particularly wish to 'take to heart', even to try to learn by heart? I select that which 'speaks to my condition', seeking to prune even what is good in favour of the best, and taking to myself the nuggets that I discover. I find I return to Luke and John more than to Matthew and Mark. I find Romans hard work, but I appreciate the flashes of light. I am endlessly fascinated and gripped by the power of the Book of Revelation. This is partly a matter of temperament, and I doubtless need to delve into the less congenial. Once in a while I make myself do it; I think this is part of my growing in God.

More personally still, as an aid to my praying, I have a kind of portable prayer kit, light enough not to burden the luggage of the traveller. I have a square cloth which I can lay over a desk or table or floor in order to claim for a short while the space which is loaned to me by my host. On it I place a candle and a picture or object or two that are 'sacramental' for me at the time – usually gifts I have been given that I continue to be particularly drawn to and that speak of love and meaning. I have a book of deeply personal prayers carved out over the years; it also includes a calendar of anniversaries and a list of the people I wish especially to keep in mind. Then I have another book of nuggety quotations, a kind of pilgrim's commonplace book – and a pile of very bad drawings of my own, for no one else's view. These are images, mostly from my dreams, which speak to me and continue to be important reminders to me on the journey. I dip into this treasure trove, again to remind myself of my own unique story and to re-member it, to allow the past to become present in such a way as to be able to move more trustingly and creatively into the future.

So I ask myself again: Does this sound too pompous or grand? Certainly, these ways of praying are irregular, never settling into a totally consistent daily or even weekly rhythm. Should I feel guilty about that or am I being too hard on myself – given that one's middle years in a complex urban world are hardly free of interruption and varied unpredictable demands? Doubtless I need to prune clutter and commitments. But as long as I have a place, however portable and temporary, as long as I have ways that help me to pray, as long as I bring myself to those ways without neglecting them for too long, as long as I am fairly fierce about the boundaries of time, then I may just have the gall to put this chapter into the post.

Being and Doing

Michael Campbell-Johnston

MICHAEL CAMPBELL-JOHNSTON is the Provincial Superior of the British Jesuits.

How do I pray? The immediate short answer is 'badly'. One of Parkinson's laws is, or should be: the more essential an activity is, the more it gets squeezed out by other less essential ones. So morning prayer gives way to that important article which needs finishing; recitation of the Office or its equivalent is eaten up by the imperative task that brooks no delay; even the Eucharist sometimes falls by the wayside. For the permanent temptation of an activist is to think he or she can go it alone. Eventually, of course, this leads to madness. I think it was Chesterton who pointed out that people who really believe in themselves are all in lunatic asylums.

Naturally justifications abound. As a religious under obedience, is not everything I do in God's service? And surely to work, as St Benedict used to say, is to pray? Hence more work, ever heavier schedules – and the incipient workaholic is born. Yet this way lies madness too. It was the American philosopher George Santayana who defined fanaticism as consisting in redoubling your effort when you have forgotten your aim. With no prayer, it is hard, perhaps impossible, to keep the aim in focus or one's work in perspective.

Usually the decline is gradual, accompanied by a growing feeling of unease and occasionally tainted with guilt. In the noviceship it was drummed into us to observe and fulfil all our 'spiritual duties' with meticulous scrupulosity. They were given pride of place on the daily agenda, taking precedence over everything else. We even used to joke that a person could be uncharitable, selfish, bigoted, rude or just insufferable but, as long as he did not miss morning oblation, he was considered a good religious.

The fundamental reason for this insistence is not hard to seek. In a famous passage in his Constitutions, St Ignatius asks his brethren to be persuaded that 'the means which unite the human instrument with God and so dispose it that it may be wielded dexterously by his divine hand are more effective than those which equip it in relation to men'. The psalmist puts it another way: 'Unless you build the house, O Lord, they labour in vain who build it' (Ps. 127:1).

But, in spite of being convinced of this truth, I doubt if I am alone in admitting that my observance of 'spiritual duties' has registered a slow decline over the years, with only occasional upward swings against the current. First the unyielding demand of studies, whether ecclesiastical or profane, soon challenged noviceship priorities. Strangely enough neither philosophy nor theology proved conducive to meditation or contemplation. The long years of formation not only fully occupied the mind but tended to drive most else out of it. At the end came the tertianship with its thirty-day retreat to restore the balance. We used to say that in philosophy we lost our reason and in theology our faith: the tertianship was invented to help us rediscover both.

But as soon as it was over, we were plunged back 'into the world' and an often hyperactive ministry that again seemed to militate against a life of prayer. Now the only chance to restore some sort of balance was the annual eight-day retreat which, in time, itself ran the risk of becoming a routine exercise in making resolutions we knew we could not keep. The net result was that nagging feeling of depression, if not guilt, already mentioned.

35

Some of us persuaded ourselves that when we retired, if that is a thing Jesuits ever do, then there would be time for prayer and we could 'make it all up'. We would be able, so to speak, to catch up with God before God caught up with us.

There is an element of caricature in all this, though I do remember one old Jesuit who rose at a minute past midnight, celebrated his Mass, recited his breviary, made his meditation and examen so that, as he put it, the decks would be cleared for his real work. Nor do I wish to suggest my own experience is universal. But again I do not think I am alone in saying that it took me some time to understand in any depth what Ignatian prayer is really about. Its mechanics are clear and the different methods in the Spiritual Exercises well explained and set out in numerous manuals. But what is the true ideal of 'contemplative in action', which, though St Ignatius himself probably never used the expression, is certainly the hallmark of his spirituality?

If it means anything, it is surely that prayer should not be separated from one's ordinary daily activity but become a integral part of it. God is to be sought and found, not by retiring from people or activities, but rather in and through them. As one modern writer on Ignatian spirituality, David Lonsdale, has put it:

> For Ignatius the flurry of daily life is where we grow towards God. Activities like prayer, worship or contemplation clearly have an important place in this wider sense of spirituality as a way of living, but theirs is not necessarily the most important place.

As well as giving a prime example of it in his own life, this apostolic prayer of finding God in all things is what St Ignatius advocated most for his followers. But he had to struggle to convince some of his early companions who were seeking long hours of private prayer for themselves or advocating them for others. He actually urged

St Francis Borgia to cut his prayer-time in half. And to another he wrote:

> It would be good to realise that not only when he prays does man serve God . . . At times God is served more in other ways than by prayer, so much so in fact that God is pleased that prayer is omitted entirely for other works, and much more that it be curtailed.

In later years, this vision was lost as successive Jesuit superiors general and general congregations institutionalized St Ignatius's charism by drawing up rules for their subjects. Their cumulative effect has been satirized as follows:

> Ignatius set up the Society of Jesus as light cavalry; Borgia turned us into infantry; Acquaviva put us into barracks; Roothan cancelled all leave; Ledochowski set up a concentration camp . . . and Pedro Arrupe said: 'Break ranks'.

It was precisely the congregation which elected Arrupe as general in 1965 that began to turn the Society back to a more genuinely Ignatian form of prayer, advocating personal responsibility and discernment rather than universal norms. There was no intention to downgrade the traditional means of seeking union with God: formal prayer, meditation, examination of conscience, hearing the Word, Eucharistic celebration. We still need to seek God in the desert, in the stillness of our soul, in our little cubby-hole under the stairs. But all these are ancillary to and supportive of the central place of our encounter with God, which is our Jesuit ministry. It follows from this that there is or should be no false division between spirituality and mission, prayer and action. In this intuition lies the originality of St Ignatius and the peculiar relevance his spirituality has for our modern world.

What does all this mean in practice? How then do I pray? The times of withdrawal are still there though neither as many nor intensive as I would like. I recognize some element of quiet and reflection is essential if I am to remain sensitive and alert to God's action in my life and ministry. But I find myself giving more and more importance to seeking God in and through that ministry itself, even in its most routine or mundane occupations. I have tried to find God in the writing of this article which I initially resisted for a whole variety of seemingly good reasons. But it has helped me come closer to God and might even help others: thus it becomes an occasion of prayer.

My present job has me visiting and listening to numerous Jesuits who open their consciences to me and describe God's action in their lives. It is often a deeply moving, sometimes humiliating, experience that easily, if one allows, brings tears of joy, gratitude or compunction. I am constantly on the move, travelling up and down the country and abroad, finding in strange places the same God in whose hands 'are the depths of the earth – the heights of the mountains are his – to him belongs the sea, for he made it, and the dry land shaped by his hands' (Ps. 95:4–5).

It is a question of letting privileged moments speak more deeply, of dwelling on them, savouring them, entering into them as, in an Ignatian contemplation, we enter into a gospel scene and make ourselves present at it. The opportunities are infinite, as varied and complex as life itself; the unaffected laughter of children, the devotion of an old couple grown together over the years, the deep companionship of friends and colleagues, the idealism and love of a boy and girl preparing for marriage, the unselfish dedication and heroism of so many voluntary workers, the generous openness and simplicity of the poor.

It is not so much raising the mind and heart to a God up or out there or even hidden within, but rather discovering him/her present all the time in the essence of things, in others, in encounters, places, events, situations, even the most unlikely. These include, of course, suffering pain, tears and anguish, for the God of surprises is lurking there too, if only we will peel away the outer layers. Child abuse, racial oppression, AIDS, torture of the innocent, exploitation of the poor, however deplorable and repugnant, can all be occasions for discovering God's love and gentleness.

I remember how a distinguished Jesuit was once asked to choose two passages in the Gospel that spoke to him best about prayer. He picked first Luke 11:1–4, where Our Lord teaches his apostles to pray and recite the Our Father. The second passage, also from Luke (10:25–37), was the parable of the Good Samaritan which, on the face of it, seems to be more about doing than praying.

But he justified his choice as follows:

> In the fourfold ministry of the Samaritan – contemplative seeing (v.33), affective response (v.33), practical caring (v.34), and sustained good even when one is absent (v.35) – I discern the way one ought to grow in prayer. Prayer is contemplative encounter with reality. Prayer is allowing one's heart and mind and emotions to be touched by what one sees. Prayer is doing the good one can do with one's talents, time, and opportunities. Prayer is learning how to create a community which will sustain the good begun. Prayer 'does' this to us – makes us contemplative and compassionate neighbours to the world as it is, in order to make the world what God intended.

This is the prayer for which I yearn and which I long to discover more. It requires a much greater openness to the Spirit than I possess at present, a deliberate effort to be attentive. Each morning we pray: 'O that today you would listen to his voice – harden not your hearts as at Meribah . . .' This is the constant struggle, the daily challenge. Yet I am encouraged by Pascal's saying that we would not be seeking God unless we had already found him. Though it is hard to shake off that guilt feeling, I sometimes dare to think I may not be praying quite so badly after all.

Prayer in the World of Television

Angela Tilby

ANGELA TILBY is a producer of documentary television programmes and a lay reader in St Albans.

I do not remember anyone teaching me to pray, but the habit of turning to prayer seems imprinted on my childhood memory. When I was small I prayed to avert evil, and to prevent family illnesses and accidents. I believed that God appreciated gratitude, but I found the world a scary place, and tended only to give thanks in order to store up a reserve of divine goodwill that I might be able to draw on in the future.

I revert to primitive prayers when flying. I feel so helpless strapped in my seat while thrusting up from the ground enclosed in a metal tube. I pray to Elijah (of the fiery chariot) and St Teresa of Avila (who travelled a lot and did not like it much). Alternatively, these days, I put my faith in statistics. The Myers-Briggs Type Indicator has led me to conclude that my *thinking* is more mature than my *feeling*. That is probably why I have a love for theology, and why the emotional content of my prayer life is almost embarrassingly direct and naïve.

I have tried to pray seriously since I was sixteen. This was when I consciously adopted an evangelical Christian faith. I was zealous for the Lord, and learned to have a 'quiet time' in the morning, which consisted of reading a portion of Scripture, looking for God's guidance within it, and making prayers of adoration, confession, thanksgiving and supplication (ACTS, for short). I used to arrive at school early and performed this ritual in the lavatories attached to the school medical room, stretching out on the floor with my bible and praying for wisdom in winning my friends for Jesus. It was not a bad way to learn the habit of prayer.

After that I became a rather bigoted Anglo-Catholic and lost something of the urgency of personal prayer in a concern for liturgical propriety. Then I always went to church on saints' days, and I longed to be able to centre my prayer life on the daily Eucharist. Since my fortieth birthday I have got bored with religious disguises and have just tried to get on with the ordinary demands of life as a theologically trained single laywoman in the world of mass communications.

I have no set practice now, though I probably pray in some way or another most days. I sometimes still long for the discipline of the monastic offices, but the timetable of my life is not regular enough to take them on properly. I have a huge respect for the Anglican priestly commitment to Morning and Evening Prayer, said, not just for oneself, but for the community in which one is set. But as a lay person I sometimes feel very much on my own. And I also have a rebellious streak. I want to do something different too often. So I compromise. I often use a form of Morning Prayer, and sometimes say Compline. I love the structure of the psalms and canticles, and the way the insights of Scripture play off each other. Some years ago when I was working on a television worship programme I wrote my own daily office for use when I had little time and was under stress. It was based on the last of the Servant Songs in Isaiah 52 and 53. The pattern of commitment and frustration, humiliation and release, spoke vividly to my experience of working as a Christian communicator in the abrasive environment of television. You work so hard, and often, it seems, for nothing. You get a beastly review for a programme you had spent your soul on, your budget is cut, you find yourself behaving unspeakably badly. 'I have spent my strength for nothing and vanity.' Yet there are tremendous compensations. There is a real community in the television world, and a commitment to human values and artistic excellence. Television has been the world in which I have had to begin to learn spiritual discipline and detachment, and, as an environment, it has been as hard and rigorous (and joyful) as any convent.

Television is fascinating but it is not glamorous. When I am exhausted I try just to sit for a while with an icon or a candle. This is terribly difficult, except at certain times of the month, when my hormones seem to predispose me for quiet. Or I use the Ignatian methods of trying to read the gospels while attending to and discerning the movements of the Spirit. Maria Boulding's book, *Gateway to Hope: an Exploration of Failure*, speaks to my experience. All successes are ambiguous. Most failures are educative. Ignatian spirituality has helped me a lot in crisis, but it is too emotionally intense for every day. I would never get to work if I prayed this way all the time. Sometimes I go through a few days of non-communication; out of sorts with God and with myself. Something always brings me back, though, and I find myself beginning with that endless cry of the mute and speechless, 'O Lord, open thou our lips.'

I think that my liking for formal, liturgical prayers, arises from a fear of God and a need to root myself in a tradition of belief that is beyond individual personality. We all have to die and to give up the relentless egoism that fuels so much of what we consciously are and do. The hard part is to make the unconscious open to God. I yearn to be able to pray in a quiet and contemplative way, but my mind is so active and distracted that it is almost impossible in normal life. Having said that, on retreat, or in certain times of grief I pray very openly and find an extraordinarily direct sense of the presence of God. I think God catches up with me when I cannot keep pace with him. He is behind as well as before, and I am always fleeing on to the next thing.

The basic issue in my prayers is always to do with trust. Can God be trusted? My heroes and heroines in Christian faith are those who have a generous and non-judgemental vision, who see the glory of what is claimed in the doctrine of the Incarnation. 'The Word was made flesh and dwelt among us, full of grace and truth.' That is so astonishing. I wish we still genuflected when the Creed gets to the Incarnation. The heart of my personal faith is in the prologue to John's gospel, the doctrine of the Word-made-flesh, containing and transforming all human birth and death.

I do not mind old-fashioned Calvinist guilt but I loathe modern, do-gooding Pelagianism, with its endless stress on improving people and berating the heritage of the Western world. Many Christians use issues like justice for the Third World and the problems of the environment as alibis to project their guilt on to other people. I am a relentless believer in democracy and technology and in the sheer materialism of the Christian Gospel. I cannot in conscience pray for a poorer, simpler life for all because I do not believe that poverty is necessarily virtuous. I like the Old Testament ideal of everyone having the means to sit 'under his vine and fig tree'. I dislike the self-conscious, self-imposed poverty that some Christian groups go in for, because it often seems to me to be a thin disguise for self-hatred. The prayers of the Church fail to recognize the quite humble aspirations of ordinary people. The Daily Office provides prayers for the 'respectable' professions – clergy, teachers, doctors – and for 'honest' manual labourers, and even 'artists', and, of course, for mothers and the unemployed. But there is nothing for lawyers, bankers, engineers, advertisers, people who work in supermarkets, actors and pop stars, sales representatives, the self-employed or working women. The false idealism implied here is persecutory, and helps keep mature Christians in a state of spiritual infantilism. By such spiritual snobbery our prayers fail to honour what is claimed by the doctrine of the Incarnation; that the Son of God enters our life *as it is*, and transforms it into the glory of heaven.

I think my work as a producer of religious programmes for television is part of a wider vocation to understand and interpret the faith for the age we live in. I often find I am trying to interpret modernity to church people at the same time as trying to make a case for faith in the world of pagan and secular assumptions. That is why I try to build bridges between science and psychology and religion. Modern cosmology is fascinating. It speaks directly to the soul of believer and unbeliever alike, and if we ignore it we impoverish ourselves by depriving ourselves of the wisdom of being creatures. I could not pray at all if I did not believe that there is a cosmic dimension to all our praying, and that we are linked to each other and to all creatures within the mind of God. Work is important to me – a God-given task. Occasionally I have powerful emotional dreams which have a numinous character, and are very often linked to a particular project or piece of work. Before I made a film about the apparitions of Medjugorje I had a dream of a landscape of mountains and seas – all black and gold. There was a great mountain with a gold peak rising out of the darkest blackness.

I pray about the films I make and the books I write. I am spiritually troubled by the upheavals in television and by both unbelief and intellectual oppression in the Church. I get quite burdened by all of this, and then I have to ring up one of my friends who will coolly remind me that I am not personally responsible for the fate of Western civilization.

I agree wholeheartedly with Dorothy Sayers when she says, 'The only Christian work is good work, well done.' I am not a workaholic, though. I take all the holidays I can. That is when I try to let God in to the pagan parts

of my soul which like gin and sunshine and dark novels
of sex and crime.

A Charismatic Way

Kristina Cooper

KRISTINA COOPER, a journalist, is the editor of 'Good News', the newsletter of the Catholic Charismatic Renewal in England. A cradle Catholic, she was renewed in her faith and had her life changed through contact with the Catholic Charismatic Renewal as a volunteer in Panama in the early 1980s.

Although I have always been a practising Catholic, I did not really start to pray until I had a conversion experience while working as a volunteer for the Church in Panama. Before that, prayer was saying an 'Our Father' and a 'Hail Mary' on my knees next to my bed before I went to sleep, and going to Mass on a Sunday. God was very far away. It was almost as if he inhabited another planet, and so prayer was something I did out of respect and habit because he was God, without really knowing why I did it.

Going to Panama brought me face to face with reality. The reality about myself and the world as it is. It was a time of great pain and confusion as I became aware that my life and its ambitions were a romantic illusion to cover up my brokenness and emptiness. I realized I had no answers to the terrible problems I saw, to the human condition and the meaning of life.

At this time I was invited to a charismatic prayer group. I hated it and thought it was smug and trivial, as people sang jolly songs and then proceeded to talk about what God had done for them in their lives that week – everything from curing backaches to getting jobs and car-parking spaces. I was furious. If God could not or would not do anything about the starving, suffering millions in the world, why would he bother with their petty lives and get them parking spaces!

Yet these ordinary people seemed to have an intimacy with God that I had never experienced, despite all the soup runs and other good works I had done. What was more, they insisted that this relationship was for everyone, not the special few, and all that you needed to do was to ask for it. So I did. Not when they were around, of course. But on my own, one night in the convent chapel where I was staying.

As I sat there, I realized I did not know what to say and it even crossed my mind that God might not exist at all. I realized that the God I had been worshipping was merely an extension of my own personality. In the end I just told him that I was prepared to change and henceforth to do whatever he wanted me to do.

Three hours later I left the chapel a changed person. I suddenly knew without a shadow of a doubt that it was all true. God was real and huge and powerful and cared for me in a personal way.

I was overwhelmed by the 'fear of the Lord' – a sudden realization of the awesomeness of God and my own arrogance and insignificance. This led to deep repentance which went on for several days but which gave way to a liberating sense of joy as I realized I had discovered my purpose for living – to get to know God better and find out what he wanted me to do with my life, instead of just expecting him to bless my ambitions.

In that chapel I experienced what is known in the Charismatic Renewal as baptism in the spirit. From that day onwards I had an overwhelming desire to know more about God. I just could not put the Bible down. It suddenly became more exciting than the most compulsive thriller. It was the same with spiritual literature. Before, I was not in the slightest interested in theology or spirituality, but since then there is hardly a book on my shelf which is not in some way tied up to God the Father, God the Son or God the Holy Spirit. I felt that I had spent so long ignoring him that I had to make up for lost time, for God is more fascinating than anything in the world.

Although my initial fervour and passion has somewhat subsided and like everyone else I find it hard to be faithful to prayer, nine years on I still love Scripture. I am no scholar and I do not understand all of it, but it does not seem to matter because I know this is his word and I love him.

The people in the prayer group in Panama were a great influence on me, and they all seemed to have something called 'quiet time' early in the morning when they spent an hour 'with the Lord'. I took this as the norm and did the same. I have more or less kept to this ever since, though I did have a time when I had a spirit of tiredness, whch lasted six months, when I just could not get up in the morning to pray. I was constantly tired and I used to get so depressed about not doing my 'prayer time' that I used to cry out to God every night to help me. I thought I was perhaps anaemic and went to the doctor. I was not. Instead, through a bizarre turn of events it turned out that it was actually a spiritual oppression, from which I was delivered instantly through prayer by a priest who was giving me spiritual direction.

But this long period of not being able to pray had got me out of my good habits and although I was no longer tired it took me eighteen months before I got back into a proper prayer schedule. This period turned out to be a time of great growth, however, because I realized that a daily prayer time was not something I achieved myself, as a good Christian, but a grace of God, and that if my particular circumstances were changed I floundered like the weak, egocentric individual I was. I realized that prayer was a relationship, not something I achieved, and that God loved me whether I prayed or not. It was the relationship that counted, not what I did.

Being the person I am, I find it hard to be still before God. Which is why my prayer is rather active – I read and meditate on Scripture, and I write in my journal.

My guilty secret is that I pray on my bed. I developed the habit when I was in Panama working in a children's home and shared a room with another girl. There was nowhere to pray so my bed became my prayer closet, and although I have tried to break the habit, past associations are so strong that I always come back to my bed. It is comfortable and I can spread all my bibles and bits and pieces around. My posture is not very spiritual either, propped up with pillows against the wall with a cup of coffee in my hand to wake me up.

To get me in the mood I put on a bit of charismatic-style praise music and sing along with it, out loud or in my heart. It is usually scripturally based or a slushy love song to Jesus. I know one is not supposed to rely on feelings but it helps me to get a bit romantic about Jesus. I do not know if St Ignatius would exactly approve, but I reckon it is not so different to what he discovered, and I have found that the warm positive feelings I get about Jesus stay with me after my prayer is over and help inspire me to serve him.

I have to watch myself, though. Early on after my conversion I clearly remember lying on my bed reading a spiritual book about dying to self and growing in love of God. I was getting warm feelings about this when there was a knock on the door and one of the children in the home came in demanding some service or other. I was very annoyed. How could I learn to die to self if the kids kept disturbing me. Then I had to laugh as I realized God was giving me the opportunity to grow in this virtue rather than just read about it.

Several years ago I was inspired by a talk given by a priest called Father Rufus Pereira, about the importance of making the Bible your home and how his life had been transformed once he started to read the Bible seriously, not just the bits he liked. As a result I have a book that enables you to read the whole Bible in a year. This is tough going when you are in Numbers or Chronicles and endless lists, but I force myself to read all of it. Sometimes I find the odd nugget there. Then I read the Mass readings of the day and look at the daily meditations in *Word Among Us*, a Catholic scripture magazine. I do this to prepare myself for Mass, because I easily become distracted and float in and out of the celebration when I am there. If I have not already read the Gospel at home, I can often leave without remembering a word that has been said.

Once again it has been a grace in my life that I have been able to go to Mass more or less daily for the last ten years. Being single and having a flexible job means that there are not the constraints many people have. Even when I was going through my hardest time, I would somehow always manage to drag myself off to Mass; I suppose because it was an action I could take to show my devotion to God even if my participation was not great and the rest of my prayer life was minimal.

I love reading the Scriptures. When something strikes me, I meditate on this, repeating it to myself, perhaps dwelling on the fact that God loves me or what Jesus has done for us. Or perhaps it might be some kind of challenge to my life and current situation. I remember once being struck by a reference to almsgiving and the importance of it. That morning someone I knew, who only got in touch with me when he wanted money, rang me up to cadge. If I had not had that word from God in the morning I would probably have give a small amount grudgingly, but because of this reading I knew that God wanted me to be generous – for my sake rather than his – to help me to detach myself from money.

As it says in Hebrews 4:12–13,

For the word of God is living and active, sharper than any

double-edged sword. It penetrates even to dividing soul and spirit, joints and marrow: it judges the thoughts and attitudes of the heart. Nothing is hidden from God's sight; everything is uncovered and laid bare before the eyes of him to whom we must give account.

I constantly find it remarkable how often the word of God speaks to me in specific situations in my life, consoling, challenging and directing me. I find as I believe the Word of God more, and act on it, my faith grows and I see God acting powerfully in my life and in the lives of others.

One of the charismatic gifts which I find helpful in prayer is the gift of tongues. Jackie Pullinger, who has a ministry to drug addicts in Hong Kong, recommends praying in tongues for fifteen minutes a day, and tells remarkable stories of her effectiveness in responding to God and his promptings when she does this. I am too lazy to do this in such a disciplined way. Instead I tend to use tongues more spontaneously, when I do not know what to say in my prayer, or particularly when I start getting terrible distractions. A quick burst of tongues usually manages to drive out erring thoughts from my brain so that I focus myself on Christ again. I also use it when I am praying with other people and do not know what to pray for but want to pray in conformity with God's will, without imposing my own ideas or agenda. It is also a great vehicle for spontaneous praise.

Those outside the Charismatic Renewal often find the use of tongues disturbing, but it is not as weird as it seems. It is just a form of non-rational prayer that comes from our spirit. I just see it as a practical way God has given us of submitting our intellects to him and a sign of total abandonment to him. The more intellectual and in control a person is, the more difficulty they tend to have with this gift because they cannot bear the foolishness of it. Sometimes when I pray this way I am tempted to think, What is this? Is this really tongues? Is this just gibberish? But then I just have to cease worrying and say, 'Whatever it is, Lord, I'm doing it for you.'

I also pray in tongues spontaneously in my head when I feel in danger or when someone says something and I cannot discern what to do. It acts then as a 'Help, Lord' prayer.

In my morning prayer time I also intercede for people and situations. One of the effects of being involved in Charismatic Renewal is deep belief in the power of prayer and intercession. I find that if I pray for someone God may ask me to be part of the solution.

I belong to a parish prayer group, which meets once a week on a Wednesday. Here we sing loud lusty hymns praising God, share readings from the Scripture, listen sometimes to a talk on the spiritual life and generally pray together. We have been meeting for seven years. Though we are a very mixed group in age, nationality and social background, through our prayer together God has moulded us into a family. As the years have passed we have come not only to share a short time of prayer every week, but also our lives and our burdens. From our communal prayer we are able also to reach out and serve in the parish.

A number of us from the prayer group are involved in catechetics. We have found from experience that the most important preparation is prayer. This means, for example, that in preparing the confirmation class, we would pray for at least thirty minutes before even starting to discuss what to do. As a result we usually find the actual work gets done in half the time and there are less disagreements and less time is wasted on endless discussions.

Time and time again I am made aware that if I do not pray I cannot cope with the work God gives me to do. This was made very clear to me one day in Panama when I was in the children's home. It had been a very hard day. I was exhausted and I had not been able to pray that morning. It was siesta time and I had a choice: pray or sleep. I slept. I woke up physically refreshed but depressed at the hard life I was having to live. I was fed up with the children and their incessant demands and decided I would not go back on duty that afternoon, so I got into my pyjamas, put a 'Do not disturb' sign on the door and said I was ill.

I sat on my bed, got out my bible, put on some soothing gentle Christian music and began to read the Scripture. An hour later, my mood had totally changed. God's words had cleansed my mind. I was in love with Jesus again and suddenly I began to love the kids again and want to go out and help them. God had changed my heart, and he continues to do this and give me the courage and the joy to go on and help bring about his kingdom.

Praying in the Carpark

Tessa Sheaf

TESSA SHEAF was born in South Africa, the daughter of an Anglican vicar. After studying social anthropology at Natal University she came to England where she taught in London. She became a Roman Catholic in her mid-twenties and after trying her vocation as a nun she got married and had eight children. She is now divorced and training as a counsellor.

I am a single parent. I have eight children, one of whom suffers from anorexia nervosa. I know I have to pray. How?

There was a time when my three youngest children were pre-school and I felt I could not pray at all. An invaluable lifeline to me then were two women friends who used to come to the house with their own pre-school children. The mothers said the rosary while the children played or squabbled as they saw fit. At that time the mystery of the Visitation took on a new meaning for me and I was made very aware of how much we need each other. We are called to journey out towards each other – perhaps not on a donkey but pushing our buggies with Sainsbury's shopping into the wastelands of modern suburban housing estates or high-rise council flats where fellow mothers may be viewing approaching childbirth with mixed feeings of fear, isolation and wonder.

Now that my youngest child has just started school I find my prayer life can take a different shape. An excellent spiritual director whom I see weekly is invaluable in guiding me and confronting me when I appear to be getting too remote from the humdrum aspects of domestic life, like dirty saucepans, odd socks and looking for shoes. At the same time he is always there to try and keep me faithful to my daily half-hour meditations with the Lord. When do I fit these in? School carparks are an ideal place to pray. After dropping the children at school in the morning – they start very early, which is a blessing – I say the Morning Office in the carpark and have my meditation time before going to Mass. Other places for prayer I have found useful are the hospital carpark when I take my daughter to the doctor or waiting in the car while one of my younger daughters has a piano lesson.

Lately in my meditations I have been following the theme of blindness and Jesus' different ways of opening the eyes of the blind – immediately, as with Bartimaeus, or gradually, as with the blind man of Bethsaida who accompanied Jesus on a journey out of the village. My director has been able to share with me my anguish when I sat with Bartimaeus and worried if the Lord would altogether pass me by. What if he never noticed me sitting there blind and begging? It was indeed a joyous moment when I discovered for myself that he is indeed 'the God who comes' – even though it may take a long time. There was no need to worry.

I meditated on the blind man of Bethsaida one recent Saturday while sitting at my son's basketball training and found I could incorporate the incessant bouncing of basketballs into my meditation. Probably Bethsaida was a pretty noisy village with much unconcerned clatter and chatter as the blind man went his way. And somehow I also found the bouncing basketball speaking to me of the crucifixion and the nails being hammered in.

It is not always so easy to find time to pray on my own when all the children are off school but I have discovered ways. I used to try, disastrously, to pray late at night – I always fell asleep. Now I have learned that if I go to bed that bit earlier and get up early, I can generally fit in half an hour's prayer before the youngest wake up and confront me with wet beds and the problems of the day.

Saying a mantra has always been for me a powerful means of keeping centred on God as the daily grind of blocked drains, blocked lines of communication, wet beds and teenage assertiveness takes its toll on my resources. It took me some time to get the courage to move from a recommended mantra that patently did not suit me (like 'Lord Jesus Christ, Son of God, have mercy on me, a sinner') to one that I found helpful. When times have been very bad – as when my marriage broke up or when my daughter's illness was particularly severe – I found all I could mutter in my heart was 'God! God! God!' This then changed to 'Oh God, you are my God, for you I long, for you my soul is thirsting.' Now I tend to focus more on a 'praise mantra' – 'May God be praised, worshipped, adored and glorified now and for ever.' I often move to a different one if things are getting tricky – when the youngest children create chaos, my daughter refuses to eat, or the house seems to be taken over by teenage boys who never stop eating and playing loud music. Then my mantra may switch to, 'Oh God, come to my aid, O Lord *make haste* to help me!' Does he? Sometimes it appears he does, at other times I feel he is wanting me to grow up a bit.

The Morning and Evening Prayer of the Church I need as faithful companions of many years' standing. They root me in the wider Church, past, present, and future, and get me out of my narrow orbit. This attachment to the Office of the Church springs from my childhood when I observed the great love my father, an Anglican clergyman in South Africa, had for his breviary. In fact he died while saying it one morning. When I say the Prayer of the Church I feel I can safely throw myself with all my pettiness into this vibrant tide of praise and supplication.

Other frequent companions in my spiritual life are characters from the Old Testament. Jacob, wrestling with the angel, became for me a reality a few years ago when I found myself wrestling with God, complaining to him and resenting what he was allowing to happen in my life. *Why* did my marriage break down? *Why* does my daughter suffer so with anorexia? *Why* do I have to be a single parent?

Currently Moses is my hero. As I hear the children's constant litany of 'Mum, it's not fair . . . you *always* let her . . . you *never* let me,' my appreciation of Moses increases. Reflection on this rock-like character surrounded by sweat and disputes in the desert steadies me as I journey through the wilderness of children's arguments about justice in its many forms. Was the distribution of manna easier than a fair sharing of tubes of Smarties or basic household tasks?, I wonder. Moses also leads me to worship in my prayer life. The 'holy ground' where he was asked to remove his shoes was at Mount Horeb. For me, 'holy ground' is people's lives. This is where I feel his presence and it elicits in me the desire to worship him.

We do as a family say the rosary in the evenings – usually. This is largely the result of the energetic encouragement of an amazing priest friend several years ago. Strangely enough, I often wonder if we should continue or not – is it relevant for the children? Are they praying? But it has become part of their evening ritual and it would be tragic to change. Nowadays I am trying to make more of the silences between the decades so that the older ones who have moved into their teens will at least get a few oases of silence in their busy days, which seem to require a background of continual music.

Prayer is for me a journey, a relationship with God, a discovery. It is exciting. Often nothing at all seems to happen and I try to find excuses to wriggle out of it. However, I just know I cannot live without it. I wrestle with God, run away from him, long and hunger enormously for him. In prayer I ask for the courage to open my heart to him and I ask him to make me brave enough to want to see like Bartimaeus.

Like Jonah I perpetually run away from the living God who makes demands on me and wants to relate to me, into a Tarshish where I look for a Jim-will-fix-it God or a Father Christmas who will take away the anguish of loneliness, divorce and rejection. Like Jonah I get indignant and fall into a rage with God when he does not fit into my plans. Like Jonah I have wanted death rather than life and I fall into a sulk in a shelter when the living God refuses to fit into my static categories as I cry from my 'belly of Sheol, from my abyss'.

The words of the *Sanctus* at Mass stick in my throat – 'God of power and might'. 'Are you a God of power and might?' I ask as I mistakenly look, like Herod, for a powerful God who will sweep into my life, spare me all pain and loneliness and change my circumstances. I mutter hopelessly, 'You are a powerless God, a tiny helpless baby, a God nailed to a cross, an insignificant piece of bread!'

I gasp breathlessly as I meet in prayer God in anguish. In the garden of Gethsemane I fall in love with the God who so painfully knows his own humanity. This God who knows his need of friends and suffers the agonies of loneliness, rejection and fear is one I can identify with, for I know he is the real God and the only one I can adore. I meet him in Gethsemane as the one who refused to short-circuit his human suffering and I know him as the Lover who embraces his beloved. He leads me from the depths of the grave of spiritual death, divorce and a broken family to start slowly to trust again. It is when I look at the lives of the people around me – often fellow divorcees – who have also wept, sweated blood and somehow crawled out of their prisons that I realize the life of each one of us is 'holy ground' where God is mysteriously wiping out fears, mending the rubble of our broken lives and leading us from darkness to light. It is then that I want to sing like Mary, 'My soul magnifies the Lord, my spirit rejoices in God my Saviour,' for then I know he does not abandon us. Although he might lead us to the grave, he does indeed bring us back. Alleluia!

Habit of a Lifetime

David Goodall

SIR DAVID GOODALL was High Commissioner to India from 1987 to 1991. A Roman Catholic, he was educated at Ampleforth and Trinity College, Oxford.

Diplomats, as Cardinal Newman observed, also have souls. As a diplomat I know that, like any other Christian, I am working in God's service and that I meet him in my neighbour. But I know too that I am preoccupied with the ephemeral: this afternoon's meeting, the telegram of instructions that must be acted on, the parliamentary question that must be answered. Add the pleasures and pressures of ordinary living, and the ephemeral all too easily takes over. I know from experience that unless I can find time to advert regularly, consciously and specifically to God's presence and seek some kind of dialogue with him, the whole supernatural dimension, the reality of the unseen life of the spirit, begins to fade.

So rather as it used to be said that the 'functioning anarchy' of India was held together by the 'steel frame' of a small but dedicated band of administrators, I try to give my own over-full and disorganized existence a 'steel frame' of regular prayer. The elements are simple, and inherited from childhood: frequent – and when circumstances and natural lethargy permit, daily – Mass and Holy Communion; a few minutes of set prayer every morning before breakfast and the same at night, before getting into bed. (Praying in bed tends to be an excellent soporific, but not much of a dialogue.)

Morning prayer has been transformed by the arrival of the simplified Divine Office in English, which my wife and I now normally recite together. (I am too tired, too faint-hearted or too lazy to do the same at night, when I say a decade of the Rosary instead.) Since I am lucky enough to live part of the time near a Benedictine monastery, I am quite often able to attend monastic Vespers, sung in Latin. I find this helps me in several ways. It is strengthening for my own faith to share the prayer of a believing community who are visibly following a Rule of Life which makes sense only because prayer itself makes sense. The antiquity and dignity of the Latin Office renew for me the timeless and unchanging dimension of God and the continuity of the community of believers; and then there is the beauty of the plainsong itself.

Reading is important, too; and even more difficult to find time for. But in principle – usually breached – I aim for a short daily spell of reflective spiritual reading: the gospels, or one of the spiritual classics. In London, this often had to be on the bus or tube; in the more privileged life of a head of mission abroad, it could sometimes be in the car on the way to the office, as an alternative to the six Indian newspapers which were my daily fare. The two books on the spiritual life which have, I think, made the most lasting impact on me have been Père de Caussade's *Self-abandonment to Divine Providence*, which vividly intensified my sense of the immediacy of God's presence and the essential simplicity of what he asks of us; and *The Way of a Pilgrim*, with its marvellous introduction to the Jesus Prayer.

Thin and inadequate I know my prayers to be; and all too often rushed and mechanical into the bargain. But I am deeply grateful to the conventional Catholic childhood which made them a matter of ingrained habit. For it is habit above all which brings me metaphorically to my knees whether I feel like praying or not, whether my frame of mind is believing or sceptical, emotional or detached, exhausted or full of spiritual and emotional energy, in a state of reconciliation or in a state of sin. And the rest, I am tempted to say, is up to God. My human will, reinforced by habit, can bring me to pray: whether and how far that prayer is fruitful is within God's gift, not mine.

But of course there is more to it than that. Further acts of will are required to put myself consciously in the presence of God. If I am with others, I think of Our Lord's words that 'where two or three are gathered together in my name, I am in the midst of you'. In church, there is the focus of Our Lord's presence in the Tabernacle, on the altar during Mass, or united with me in Communion. Alone, I think of God as 'compared to the air we breathe'; of Our Lord's words in St Matthew, 'When you pray, go to your private room, shut yourself in, and so pray to your Father who is in that secret place', and of Eckhart's doctrine that by the Incarnation Our Lord not only became 'a man like us', but entered that 'inner realm of the human heart' – of each human heart – which Eckhart calls 'the ground of the soul' and so is present in the core of each of us.

This act of awareness – 'placing myself in the presence of God' – is itself an act of prayer which, it seems to me, sanctifies whatever follows, whether it is participation in the liturgical prayer of the Church, the Rosary, the Office or the contemplative prayer which St Francis de Sales calls 'the prayer of the heart'. Equally, I believe that it sanctifies my distractions; and not only ordinary distractions, but also the rebellious, suffering, embittered or disbelieving thoughts which may be uppermost in my mind when I try to pray. I have often been grateful for the words of the wise Carthusian who wrote:

The *fiat* God asks of us when we suffer is not the *fiat* of insensibility, but of suffering. When our heart is torn and continues to be so, we must give it to him as it is. Later, when peace returns, we will give it to him at peace. What he wants is for us to give ourselves to him as we are. If there is anything to be put right he will do that, because we shall have handed ourselves over completely to him.

What is said here about suffering is, I believe, equally true of other forms of resistance to, or alienation from, God. Suffering, in a sense, seems a natural subject for prayer, for laying before the Lord: 'Come to me, all you that labour and are burdened, and I will give you rest.' But about anger, downright disbelief or persistence in serious sin? For me, these too are material for dialogue with the Lord. If prayer is 'the raising up of the mind and heart to God', then the thoughts which fill the mind and heart must be raised up too, even if they are perverse or malign. When my will is in conflict with what I believe to be God's will, sometimes the conflict is so deep that I cannot even say with sincerity, 'Bend my heart to your will, O God'; but at least I can show him the conflict; perhaps if I cannot bring myself to ask him to change my will, I can at least tell him that I would like to want to ask him to do so – but just cannot.

What goes for conflict of wills, goes too for doubt and disbelief. Just as there are times when the presence and reality of God are almost palpable, so there are times, and not infrequently, when the existence of a personal God and the Christian view of this life as a preparation for Eternity appear to be a grand illusion. From the perspective of many of the most articulate people among whom we live and whose opinions on other matters we respect, prayer is simple escapism: a form of systematic wish-fulfilment, of taking refuge from reality in a comfortable world of one's own private creation. Even from a Christian perspective, the old simplicities can easily look like 'fundamentalism': and there is the nagging worry that prayer is no more than a refined form of self-indulgence – especially when it fails to express itself in action. So it is easy to get into a vicious downward spiral of doubting the validity of prayer and being unable to turn to God for help because to do so would be to rely on the validity of an illusion.

Here again, habit comes to the rescue: I compose myself to pray because praying, however haltingly or half-heartedly, has become automatic; and once I start to pray I can lay my disbelief before the Lord along with all my other troubles and weaknesses, in the knowledge that, if God is truth, the truth is what he wants, including the truth about my own inability to believe. He is not looking for forced intellectual submission at the price of intellectual integrity. And, in the words of that wise Carthusian, 'if there is anything to be put right, he will do that, because we shall have handed ourselves over completely to him'.

In my non-formal prayer I still follow the advice in the college prayer book I was given at school: 'Talk to our Lord quite simply, lay before him our needs and desires, both spiritual and temporal, and ask him to help us in our daily difficulties and temptations.' It follows that a good deal of my prayer is petitionary: for those I love, for those who suffer, for the Church and those who struggle to hold and teach the faith, and of course for myself. I am conscious of how easy it is to use prayer as an alternative to action, and I know that I am resistant to the changes – the repentance – to which prayer should lead. All too clearly I recognize in myself the seed that fell among thorns, that growing up 'choked with cares and riches and pleasures of this life, yields no fruit'. But how odd it would be to have access to Our Lord and not put my hopes and needs in front of him. Often I do not need to put the petition into words: it is enough to bring the person prayed for into the scope of my awareness of God's presence; to 'remember him or her before God' – who knows both what I wish for the person concerned (or for myself) and what is best for us. And there is a special place for prayers to Our Lady. When I turn to her I am conscious not just of a humanly maternal intimacy, but also that I am praying very much as a Catholic, out of the heart of a specifically Catholic tradition of reverence for Mary: and I hope never to lose the habit, inculcated at school, of saying the *Memorare* at the outset of a journey.

But at the heart of prayer is silence. So after Communion or reading a passage from the gospels, I try for a little while to find the Lord in silence, perhaps before a crucifix, by reflecting on the gospel story I have just read – how vividly, for example, one can hear the voice of Jesus in the disciples' account of their meeting with him on the road to Emmaus, or in his recounting of the parable of the prodigal son – or just in relaxing and presenting him, however briefly, with a receptive mind and heart. And then I try to model myself on St Anselm, who summed it all up a long time ago:

> Come now, insignificant man, fly for a moment from your affairs, escape for a little while from the tumult of your thoughts. Put aside now your weighty cares and leave your wearisome toils. Abandon yourself for a little to God and rest for a little in him.
>
> Enter into the inner chamber of your soul, shut out everything save God and what can be of help in your quest for him and having locked the door seek him out. Speak now, my whole heart, speak now to God: 'I seek your countenance, O Lord, your countenance I seek.'
>
> Come then, Lord my God, teach my heart where and how to seek you, where and how to find you.

For most of the time we live and think on the surface of ourselves; on what Bernanos called the thin, superficial topsoil of life which gives us the impression of genuine existence. These words of St Anselm, charged with the intensity of first-hand experience, are for me a constant reminder of the need to penetrate below the surface in search of the God who is at the heart of things.

In the Company of the Divine Guest

Olu Abiola

OLU ABIOLA is leader of the Aladura International Church and joint president of the Council of Churches for Britain and Ireland. He lives in a council flat in Brixton, London.

I am from the Yoruba tribe in the western part of Nigeria. The Yorubas believe that full responsibility for all the affairs of life belongs to their Deity; their own part is to do as they are ordered through the priests and diviners whom they believe to be the interpreters of the will of the Deity. Through all the circumstances of life, through all its changing scenes, its joys and troubles, it is the Deity who is in control. Before a child is born, the oracle gives directions about it; at every stage of life – puberty, betrothal, marriage, taking up a career, building a house, going on a journey – man is in the hands of the Deity whose dictate is law, and who is waiting on the other side of this life to render rewards, good or bad.

The Yorubas do little abstract thinking. The picture of the Deity, therefore, is of a Personage, venerable, majestic, aged but not ageing, with a greyness which commands awe and reverence. He is *Alewilese* (He who alone can speak and accomplish), *Alagbara julo* (The all-powerful), *Arinu r'ode*, *Olumo okan'* (He who sees both the inside and outside of man's heart), *Oyigiyigi Oba aiku* (The mighty, Immovable Rock that never dies).

My traditional belief makes it necessary for me never

to lose the recollection of God's real presence for a single moment of my life. God dwells in us. Everyone in a state of grace bears the most high God in him. St Paul of the Cross writes:

> Faith tells us, that our heart is a large sanctuary, because it is the temple of God, the dwelling-place of the Holy Trinity. Often visit this sanctuary, see that the lamps are alight – that is to say, faith, hope, and charity. Frequently stir up your faith when you're studying, working, or feeding, when you go to bed and when you rise and make aspirations to God.

I like being with God and talking to him. I carry him about in the back of my mind, so that I may turn to him in case of need. I pray every moment of my life, in my work, in my thought and in my worship. 'The shortest road to attain to divine charity', says Louis of Grenada, 'is to raise our hearts to God by our strong affections and by desires that are on fire for his love, by conversing with him with respectful confidence and keeping ourselves recollected in his presence.'

I talk to God about everything because I believe that he is my Father and also my Friend whose love can never fail. I cannot be happy with him if I am holding something back, refusing to bring into the open and to discuss with him some petty selfishness. It may be obstinacy, or it may be shame; the prodigal son was obstinate, and then ashamed, but when he summoned up courage to swallow his pride and come home and confess, his father welcomed him with love and forgiveness.

I start my prayer with confession, therefore – of my inadequacies, intolerance, anger, selfishness. 'For all have sinned and come short of the glory of God.' I then proceed to ask for forgiveness. No one can escape from sinning, because we are all born in sin. Man is evil in heart, corrupt and perverse in his ways, depraved in mind. All have come short of the glory of God and I am in no way exempted.

Then I say the prayer of adoration. I adore God the

Father, Son, and Holy Spirit: acknowledging the sovereignty of the Loving God, honouring the Risen Christ, and imploring the presence of the Holy Spirit. In adoration, I recount the attributes of God and experience of their manifestation, both in my life and in the lives of others as expressed in the Bible (e.g. Exod. 34: 5–8; Rev. 7:9–12).

After adoration comes my prayer of thanksgiving to God for the Amazing Grace that was made possible through the sacrificial death of my Lord and Saviour, Jesus Christ. I was born into a deep-rooted, active and disciplined Christian family, but without the Amazing Grace which has sustained, strengthened and guided me, I should have been lost and forgotten. I also thank him for the ineffable love and goodness he showers on me, my family, friends and the whole world.

Finally, I engage in supplication and intercession for myself, my family, relations, friends, the suffering world and the divided Church of God. In all these prayers, I make extensive use of the book of Psalms, using those which are relevant. My favourites are Psalms 8, 19, 23, 24, 27, 46, 91, 121, 130, 136 and 150.

It is said that prayer is the Christian sword, but it might be more accurate to say that it is one edge of a two-edged sword, the other edge being the practice of fasting. This was certainly a common practice of the early Christians, and it is a sign of how much is lacking in Christianity today that Christians generally do not fast. In my own understanding of spiritual life, fasting is a necessity because of the ministry of deliverance and spiritual development. 'For we wrestle not against flesh and blood, but against principalities, against powers, against the rulers of the darkness of this world, against spiritual wickedness in high places' (Eph. 6:12). I fast as well as pray in order that my prayers might be effective.

In my busy life, I am not alone. I do not work without God, because he never leaves me as long as I try my best to do his will and listen to his voice. When I go into church to join in some service or to say some private prayers, I carry with me my tabernacle, bear within me the Real Presence; therefore all I have to do will be done in the company of the divine Guest. I must not become immobile in static adoration, because my duties oblige me to work, nor must I work frantically, without an aspiration of adoring love, for I bear a Guest within me, I am a living ciborium.

My favourite hymn:

> What a fellowship, what a joy divine,
> Leaning on the everlasting arms;
> What a blessedness, what a peace is mine,
> Leaning on the everlasting arms.
>
> Oh, how sweet to walk in this pilgrim way,
> Leaning on the everlasting arms;
> Oh, how bright the path grows from day to day,
> Leaning on the everlasting arms.
>
> What have I to dread, what have I to fear,
> Leaning on the everlasting arms;
> I have blessed peace with my Lord so near,
> Leaning on the everlasting arms.
>
> *Chorus* Leaning, leaning,
> Safe and secure from all alarms;
> Leaning, leaning,
> Leaning on the everlasting arms.

It is the experience of all Christians, the greatest as well as the feeblest, that there are constant ups and downs in prayer. Sometimes God seems very near, very real; sometimes he is distant and prayer is an uphill task. There is therefore no reason to be discouraged if at times we do not seem to get much out of it so long as we believe that God 'is able to do exceeding abundantly above all that we ask or think, according to the power that worketh in us'. Unto him be praise and glory forever. Amen.

Prayer on the Move

Joyce Huggett

JOYCE HUGGETT is a prolific and bestselling writer. Her books include Listening to God, Open to God *and* The Smile of Love. *After many years serving in parish ministry with her husband in Nottingham, she now lives in Cyprus.*

Like my life at present, my prayer is always on the move. Before my husband and I left Nottingham where we had lived for nineteen years, my prayer was characterized by a sustaining rhythm: an hour of stillness in my prayer room most days, a quiet day a month in a convent conveniently near my home, and an annual retreat. This is my preferred rhythm. But now that my settled home has been replaced by a nomadic existence, I have been forced to change my pattern of prayer.

I planned this chapter in the transit lounge of Athens airport. I started writing it at the Leonardo da Vinci airport in Rome and I put the finishing touches to it in a retreat centre in Wales just before embarking on a thirty-day retreat.

At the time of writing, David and I are engaged in an itinerant ministry which, in the space of six months, will take us, among other places, to Cyprus and Israel, Italy and Austria, Tasmania and New Zealand as well as various parts of England. Consequently, the cherished rhythm has been abandoned and my props, like my prayer room and spiritual director, have been removed. I am in transit. This challenging new chapter of my life has forced me to re-examine what I mean by prayer and to select certain components which are relevant to my present lifestyle. Four stand out. When these are in place, like legs of a chair, they bring stability no matter where I am or what I am doing. When one goes missing, the chair wobbles.

First and foremost there is the leg of contemplation. By that I mean that mystery which never ceases to amaze me, that Almighty God, like a loving parent gazing on his or her child, contemplates me in love. For me, prayer begins with this awareness. I try to tune into it daily.

Sometimes I do this by relishing the psalmist's observation: 'As a father is tender towards his children: so is the Lord tender to those that fear him' (Ps. 103:13). Sometimes, by drinking in God's promise expressed through Isaiah: 'As one whom his mother comforts, so I will comfort you' (Isa. 66:13). Sometimes by recalling memories of parents I have observed in the various countries I visit – like the father I once watched on a beach. His child had just begun to walk. Clothed only in a nappy, it was clearly enjoying the warmth of the Cyprus sunshine, the refreshing breeze blowing in from the sea and the sheer freedom of being able to choose between paddling in the inviting Mediterranean or walking on the firm, wet sand. With obvious delight it zigzagged drunkenly from the sea to the sand and back again, unaware that its father was looking on with equal delight, amusement and awe. The psalmist awakens in me the awesome realization that God loves me like that.

So prayer, for me, begins by taking my place at Jesus' feet like Mary or coming to God like Moses to whom God said: 'Here is a place near me' (Exod. 33:21). This reminder draws me, as with a gravitational pull, into the depths of God's love and stirs up inside me the dormant desire to contemplate him with reciprocal love, adoration and worship. Even when that desire has been reawakened, it frequently takes time to let go of the clutter which so easily obscures my vision of him, so much of my prayer time seems to.be taken up with deliberate attempts to hand over to God the pressures and dead-lines, the anxieties and excitements which constantly clamour for attention: to become still. In the words of Peter, to 'cast all my cares on him, knowing that he cares about me' (1 Pet. 5:7).

Playing quiet music helps this unwinding process, so I keep beside me a number of cassettes whose music helps me to sense the presence of God – my books *Reaching Out* and *Open to God* have been specially designed to bring people into stillness. While 'tuning the instrument at the gate' in this way, to borrow John Donne's phrase, I am often aware of the phases of prayer described by Bishop Stephen Verney. In the first phase it is 'me and him'. In the second, the dynamic sees a subtle change – it becomes 'him and me'. In the third phase it is 'just him'.

This progression has become increasingly important to me over the years. That is one reason why I keep a prayer journal. I often begin my prayer by writing a letter to God in which I 'tell it like it is' – explaining how I really feel and why. Hiding nothing. During this phase, quite unashamedly, I take the centre of the stage: 'me and him'. Writing in this way dislodges all kinds of emotions and frees me to move on to phase two where I move to the wings and God takes his rightful place centre stage: 'him and me'. Praying an abbreviated ver-sion of the Jesus Prayer helps me to make that transition – particularly when I pay attention to my breathing. As I breathe in, I say the first part of the Name: Je-. As I breathe out, the second: –sus. This way my distracted, fragmented thoughts seem to be rounded up and I find myself ready to focus on God with all my senses – expect-ing to hear him or see him, sense him or feel his pres-ence.

This is the stage of prayer where slow reading of the Scriptures comes into its own. I read a few verses as slowly as possible, pausing when a word or a phrase, a sentence or a pen-picture captures my attention or imagination. Then I savour it and feast on it, particularly if it conjures up a picture of Jesus, like these familiar verses:

> [Jesus] took his place at table . . . Then he took bread, and when he had given thanks, he broke it and gave it to them, saying, 'This is my body given for you; do this in remembrance of me'. He did the same with the cup after supper, and said, 'This cup is the new convenant of my blood poured out for you.' (Luke 22:14–20)

This is the place, too, where I might contemplate what lies before me, expecting it to become an icon – a window into heaven. If I am praying in an aeroplane, for example, the mountains or the shimmering sea, the cauliflower clouds or the cloudless sky might be the fingers which point me to God. If I am enjoying a prayer walk, dew-drops on an abandoned seagull's feather or the bronze leaves of a beech tree in autumn might trigger praise of the Creator. If I am in a prayer room or a church, a cross or a stained-glass window might provide the visual focus I sometimes need to become aware of the presence of Almighty God. When using such prayer aids, I sometimes feel as though I am stepping on an escalator which conveys me into the felt presence of the God who loves me.

There used to be a time when I prayed like this for an hour a day while the remaining twenty-three hours seemed strangely God-less. One reason why I have entitled this chapter 'Prayer on the Move' is that my prayer is always changing. Increasingly I am recognizing the need to 'practise the presence of God', to use Brother Lawrence's phrase; to move out of this time of sustained stillness into the maelstrom without losing that sense of being enfolded by love.

For this reason, though I am as yet a novice, I am trying to take seriously the advice Brother Lawrence gave to those who begged him to divulge the secret of his round-the-clock in-touchness with God: to recognize that my prayer place is portable since my oratory is my heart, to cast God-loving glances and to talk to him in the middle of what Richard Foster calls the 'muchness and manyness' of full and stimulating days, to punctuate such days with 'little solitudes' when, for a few seconds, I can remind myself of God's promise: 'Never will I leave you; never will I forsake you' (Heb. 13:5).

I am training myself to become more acutely aware that God is with me every moment of every day. It is only my forgetfulness that prevents me from being aware of him. For this reason prayers like this one, from David Adam's *The Cry of the Deer Triangle*, often find an echo in my heart:

> You, Christ, are here and with me now . . .
>> open my eyes to your presence,
>> open my ears to your call,
>> open my heart to your love,
>> open my will to your command.
>
> Christ, you have promised you will be with me 'always, to the end of the age'. My imagination may fail, but your presence is real. My eyes may be dim, but you are still there.
>
> Christ, I call upon your name, for you are with me. I am never alone, never without help, never without a friend, for I dwell in you and you in me.

Connectedness is the second leg of my prayer chair. The third is compassion.

Contemplatives are sometimes accused of being self-indulgent escapists – of being so heavenly minded that they are no earthly use. In defence, in the light of my own experience, I can only underline Jean Vanier's claim in his book *I Walk with Jesus*:

> When I walk with Jesus,
> He always leads me to the poorest,
> the lowliest and the lost,
> so that I may open my heart to them . . .
> To welcome the poor means

to become their friend,
to live a heart-to-heart relationship with them,
to listen to them, to touch them with respect,
to discover their beauty,
and reveal this beauty to them,
to love them just as they are.

In my experience, to be with Christ in the way I have
described is to discover that Christ-like compassion is
contagious. I cannot claim to be doing anything big, like
working with the hospice movement or organizing soup
kitchens, though I take a keen interest in such initiatives
and support some to the best of my ability. Instead, my
husband and I are engaged in helping a different kind
of poor – those who work for peace and justice in the
countries I have mentioned and elsewhere. In rescuing
others, they themselves frequently need a helping hand
or a listening ear. This we seek to give them. This is one
of the ways in which we try to live our prayer.

Compassion overflows, too, in the form of intercessory
prayer, by which I mean coming into God's presence
with people on my heart; people I know and love and
those I have never met but for whom I feel I carry a
burden.

There is special value, I find, in meeting with like-
minded Christians to intercede for others – especially
where the group is so conscious of the omniscience of
God that it is content to hold people and situations to
God in silence, allowing him to be God. I value such
Christian groups more than ever now that my husband
and I no longer belong to any one parish. In fact, community is the fourth leg of my prayer chair.

Retreats and quiet days will, I imagine, always be
important to me. But I am learning just how much I need
people's friendship and fellowship, that interdependence
is a gift we should not despise. In particular, I value the
opportunity to worship with others, especially in the
context of the Eucharist which is a vital part of my

prayer. Here, together with other pilgrim people, I receive with gratitude food for the journey – the Body and Blood of the Lord. And that final liturgical charge to go out in the power of the Spirit to live and work for God rarely ceases to thrill me. It seems to sum up what, for me, prayer is all about.

Path to the Still Centre

Laurence Freeman

*LAURENCE FREEMAN is the spiritual successor of John
Main. He is the director of the World Community for
Christian Meditation and a Benedictine monk of the Monastery
of Christ the King in London. His books include* Light
Within, The Selfless Self *and* A Short Span of Days.

How do I pray? If you were to ask a musician how he
played he would probably reply, 'By practising.' Anything that occupies us as a whole person requires regular
practice. We are always beginners at anything that is
real. I feel I pray by learning to pray.

The musician, if pressed for more, would then perhaps
mention his teacher, as this would describe succinctly his
school or tradition of playing. Although prayer, like
music, is essentially universal and can transcend all bar-
riers within and between people, it too falls into schools
of spirituality. My own teacher was John Main, who first
learned to meditate from an Indian monk, and then, after
himself becoming a Benedictine monk, rediscovered the
same tradition of the mantra which his teacher had
taught him, in the 'pure prayer' of the Christian desert
fathers.

The mantra is a sacred word or phrase which is
repeated continuously with love and fidelity throughout
the half-hour of the meditation period. All thoughts and
other mental activities are left behind in this work. All
meditation aims to bring the person, mind and body, to
silence, stillness and simplicity of spirit by the means of

an inner 'object of attention'. The act of attention is the inner sacrifice and the work of paying attention is the school of letting go. The utter simplicity of such a way to joy and peace makes one laugh. God seduces us by simplicity. Perhaps one person's simplicity is another's complexity and another's impossibility.

They say that the teacher appears when the student is ready. I was introduced to meditation at a crucial moment of faith in my early twenties, when I had out-grown the forms and beliefs of my childhood and was trying hard to relate my personal experience to 'God'. This opportune timing remains a most concrete example for me of how prayer, grace and faith are interrelated and are all pure gift.

The guru or spiritual teacher is, I think, a vital element in learning to pray, and so it was with me, but he or she fulfils that role by pointing beyond himself, as Jesus did by pointing to the Father. The guru, like the saint or sage, teaches by presence and example rather than by dogma and ritual; and so he reveals prayer as the inner journey of self-knowledge and self-transcendence.

For the Christian the guru is Jesus, who was asked by his disciples to teach them to pray. All Christian prayer, then, whatever its school of spirituality, is united in obedience to this master's teaching. It is meant to bring us to that same experience of Jesus which enabled him to know who he was, where he came from and where he was going. Meditation could not be Christian if it were not in essential harmony with what Jesus taught about prayer.

It also has to make sense, through the level of personal experience, of the idea that the mind of Christ dwells in us and that the Spirit unites us to God through its bound-less cry of love. The mantra seems to me to be rooted in Jesus' teaching on prayer in the Sermon on the Mount, not only because of Jewish practices of repetive prayer, but because it makes real to me what Jesus taught about interiority, trust, brevity, mindfulness and letting go of anxiety in prayer.

In meditation I find a way of moving beyond external religiosity into the solitude of the inner room; of leaving behind the babble of many words (however beautiful) in the confidence that all human needs are known to God even before they are known to us. In seeking to find the centre of our being we must combine the qualities of play and work, freedom and discipline: in the playful work of meditation I find a way to leave anxiety behind so as to set the mind upon the Kingdom before everything else. This does not mean that meditation is a quick fix for all our problems, but it does wonderfully change the ground on which we face them: from the ground of the ego to the ground of being.

The challenge of meditation, wherever one may be on the journey (and one may be at different levels simultaneously), is its simplicity. This is so, I think, because simplicity is unity and there is no greater hunger in us than to find this experience of unity beyond our separate egos. In prayer, we move beyond self-consciousness. But we cannot say there is only one way to come to this. That is why there is nothing more foolish than rivalry between ways of prayer.

Meditation does seem to me, more and more, to be a wonderfully simple and accessible spiritual path for leaving self behind and for coping with the complex dangers of self-deception and egotism in ourselves and others. It has been a miracle of my life to see so many ordinary men and women find the contemplative dimension of their lives by this way. I know it is not the only way, but I feel it is important to have a way to which we are committed. How can we come to true tolerance and respect for the ways to which others are committed, unless we are committed to a way ourselves? This paradox between commitment and tolerance lies at the heart of the inter-faith question which is the deepest challenge before the world today. How can Christians begin to meet this challenge without learning, somehow, to pray deeper than words? I know from sharing in the growth of others that meditation broadens tolerance and deepens compassion.

As a child I can remember, like many people, powerful experiences of God for which no conceptual software of understanding was yet loaded into my brain. Later the software tended to supersede the experience. As the ego develops in a person, prayer tends to become more ego-centric, and we can only recover the primary experience of God by learning to transcend our egotism.

This can be painful as only a crisis of faith can be. Recently I was talking to a meditator from the Philippines who told me how she had come to meditation. A young nephew of hers had been kidnapped and held for ransom. She and her prayer group joined with others around Manila to pray for the boy's safe release. They prayed round the clock and bombarded heaven with the most heartfelt prayers. When, a week later, the boy was murdered, she faced the most intense crisis of faith: whether to hate God or to love God more deeply, to give up prayer or to pray more deeply.

Petitionary prayer is not the heart of prayer. Crises of growth, such as the one I have described, have served to help me understand why St Isaac of Syria said that we only begin to pray when we stop praying. I think of this now by seeing prayer as a great wheel which turns the cart of our life ever godwards. Part of it is always touching the ground; prayer must be rooted in daily reality. The outer rim is held together by the spokes; each spoke is a distinct form of prayer. Different spokes for different folks. The spokes themselves are united at the hub where there is stillness. For Christians, the hub is the prayer of Jesus in his union with God to which the Spirit guides us.

Meditation is in one sense another spoke of the wheel. In another sense, as the contemplative experience that takes us beyond all forms, it is the meeting-point with the one who teaches us to pray by praying in, and with, us. It is the point where the spoke meets the hub. This point is one of union and, glimpsed even once, we know that it is the meaning of life.

I meditate at regular times each day, and usually integrate these half-hours of silence and stillness with the divine office or the Eucharist. Even when travelling across time-zones I try to keep to these regular times because they are precious and necessary for me. They teach me that the journey of prayer is made both on the micro and macro scale; not only are the daily wounds healed but the whole life-pattern is being resolved as well. My aim in praying at these set times is to learn to pray at all times. It is to expand temporary enlightenments into a continuous awareness of the presence of God. I have found that the more self-conscious this aim is, the less it can be realized. Prayer remains, like music, an art which achieves its excellence in peaks of grace that are essentially effortless.

The mantra offered me a simple way to this effortlessness, because by becoming rooted in the heart it can continue unaffected by irritability when waiting in a supermarket queue, or by frustration when missing a plane or having one's hopes dashed. Meditation is about remaining rooted in the centre of being, deeper than external trials as well as all surface moods and waywardness. It is not, as every meditator knows, what happens during the meditation period that matters. The fruits of the spirit manifest themselves in ordinary daily realities.

One of the greatest gifts of prayer is that it makes everything sacred. This has also made me realize that there is nothing, not even the most pious work, including prayer, which cannot become an obstacle to the realization of God if the ego attempts to take it over. Prayer is the heart of religion precisely because it goes to the root of egotism which is the basis of all separation and conflict.

In the experience of God the duality between sacred

and profane is dissolved. To have everything reveal and celebrate God is, I feel, the aim of the monastic life, and this is why the monk's life revolves around prayer. It is also why meditation reveals and fulfils the monastic archetype in every person and why this self-discovery begins the experience of true community. I do not think of meditation as a 'higher' form of prayer meant for a spiritual élite. If anything, meditation, like monasticism, is meant for those with the bigger egos.

From the beginning I have realized that I always meditate in community, however solitary the place or mood. From this point, we are able to enter that experience of God which comes from seeing and sharing in the spiritual growth of others. This means the tremendous grace of friendship, encouragement and solidarity: everything that the New Testament means by *koinonia*, communion, or the Buddhists by the *sangha*, community. It has also meant the discovery that the ego gets stronger and more disruptive even as people are drawn closer in this way. But meditation has deepened my belief in the eventual triumph of the spirit of unity.

Really, as the musician also knows, it comes down to perseverance. The only thing that counts is commitment, as a famous atheist once said. Perseverance takes one through times of faith-deepening doubt, of hope-fulfilling despair and of joy-expanding loss. There are always timely glimpses, through the mists, of the simple and present reality of that ocean of bliss in which human life unfolds. The saints and sages see this more constantly than most of us, even in their suffering. But we all need the personal experience of this reality, and never more so than today.

In our ego-tormented, economics-obsessed consumerism, we need the other-centredness of meditation more urgently than ever before. We need a middle way of prayer between the aggressive certainties of fundamentalism and the vagaries of New Ageism. Contemplation is the antidote for the one and the corrective for the other.

The Church, together with the other great religious traditions, must be responsible for teaching this universal way. It must show that the narrow path opens us to what is boundless, and that the entrance to it is free and simple.

Because spiritual hunger today is so great there is the danger of it being treated like a demand for a commodity. Only the great religious traditions of our human family can prevent the consumerization of spirituality. Only they can prevent the way beyond egotism from becoming another of the ego's toys and, instead, further the marriage of contemplation and responsible action. I feel I can only pray today within an awareness of these contemporary urgencies.

Meditation works, simply and subtly, by letting the centre of our consciousness drop from the ego into the true self. Only when we stop thinking of prayer as if it were 'my prayer' can we begin to glimpse what prayer really is. From this new vantage point we see the world with a unified vision. It is, therefore, the most direct way to change the world.

Prayer for Others

Martin Israel

MARTIN ISRAEL is a medical pathologist and priest-in-charge of Holy Trinity with All Saints, London. He is an experienced writer and broadcaster.

My relationship with God has usually been wonderfully direct. Even as a child I was aware of the divine presence close to me, so that open conversation with him seemed quite natural. I did not come from a very religious family. I suspect that my mother had inner yearnings but these were kept in the background of a busy family life and the rather neurotic personality she possessed. My father was destructively agnostic about all things spiritual until shortly before his death at the age of ninety, and I found his insistence on material comforts disagreeable and frustrating.

Despite this non-Christian family background, Jesus himself came to me at a very early age and showed me the path I was to traverse. I am, I might say, enormously grateful for the care my parents took of me, giving me a good education which fitted me for later medical studies. On this basis I attained a more mature spirituality, enabling me to do a large amount of counselling and retreat conducting, and culminating in my ordination to the Anglican priesthood in my middle years.

As an only child, I led of necessity a solitary life, and the presence within could easily have been dismissed as a wish-fulfilling fantasy had it not given me the courage to persist, even though I often found myself in a very

alien environment. This suppport not only made me continue but also showed me the way forward, despite often
being met with blank incomprehension. My intercourse
with God was essentially silent. During periods of stress
and hostility, when I needed calmness and reassurance,
I knew the divine presence in the heart.

When inspiration poured from me in counselling, lec-
turing or writing, the same presence has dominated my
head. The Orthodox prayer of the heart – 'Lord Jesus
Christ, Son of God, have mercy on me, a sinner', often
contracted by the believer into the simple, 'Jesus, Jesus,
Jesus' – was a natural accomplishment of my spiritual
life. I required no repeated request like the one recorded
in Luke 18:13 to bring me to the divine presence, but I
never lost sight of the publican within myself who
needed unceasing absolution.

As I grew more accustomed to spiritual life in the adult
context of service in the world as a confirmed celibate,
the divine presence made my way increasingly clear to
me. Having no family responsibilities, I was brought to
see the whole world, or at least that portion in my
immediate vicinity, as my family. In this respect Jesus'
ministry, confined to Palestine, became the great example
laid before me of service to the world in a restricted
context. Later, an individual practice of intercessory
prayer was to underline this 'minute particularity' (to
quote William Blake) of my work. The Holy Spirit within
me showed me my path of prayer, also indicating its
importance for the coming of God's kingdom in my own
limited milieu. To whom much is given, much is also
expected: otherwise the gift within oneself becomes sour
and distasteful.

To me prayer is entering wholly, without any outside
distraction, into the presence of God. I have always
known God as a personal being of immense love, and
when I come fully to him, I converse with him as directly
as I do with a person alongside me. The nearest I myself
get to a 'mantra' is the repetition of clauses of the Lord's

Prayer, which I direct to God with clear, undistracted attention. It is in the early morning that my attention is especially keen, for my mind, usually refreshed by a good sleep, seems to have an immaculate clarity about it. Once I have spoken to God in the prayer that Jesus taught his disciples – still the greatest enunciated prayer in my experience – I speak to the divine presence in short personal ejaculations of praise and aspiration. Then I am silent.

Next I say the Office, with special emphasis on the Bible readings. I have always loved Holy Scripture, both Old and New Testaments, not in a narrow literalistic way, but as an eternal commentary on the human condition, and therefore relevant to me also in my various conflicting moods. The Psalms are an unrivalled source of spiritual and emotional experience; I read the psalm for the day aloud to myself, while meditating on the Old and New Testament lessons in silence. These are as good a basis for meditation as anything I have come across, but one needs a free spirit to enjoy them in their totality.

All this is simply a preliminary, albeit a vital one, to the work of prayer. It puts me in a right frame of mind for my intercourse with God and the work he has in store for me. All this is done soon after I awaken, shave, and clothe myself, long before my cold breakfast.

Now I am quiet before God, and in the stillness know him as friend and mentor. The consciousness rises from the lower part of the body to the top of the head, and I rejoice in the immeasurable gentleness of his embrace. I then speak briefly, either vocally or simply mentally, depending on the circumstances, asking that certain character defects may be healed, or at least ameliorated. Thus I ask to be more loving, compassionate and charitable; more patient, forbearing and long-suffering; more tolerant, humble and self-controlled; more enduring, courageous, and with a greater sense of humour; more faithful, forgiving, and aware of the divine presence, so that the ego is put into its right place as servant and not

master, and does not look for rewards and praise; all this
to the end that my life on earth may help in the coming
of God's kingdom in the world. These petitions recur
frequently, reminding me how far I am from serving the
community as perfectly as I should. As time goes by, I
am aware of subtle character-changes attending situations
where previously I would have behaved selfishly or
impatiently; whenever I notice this I give thanks to God
forthwith, lest complacency lead me back into old ways
of behaviour. After this period of confession and petition
comes a still deeper silence that may last some time (of
course one does not measure these things). And then
the Holy Spirit quickens my mind to remember the large
list of people whom I know need divine assistance.

The prime mover in intercession is God, not us. Dame
Julian of Norwich was well instructed when she wrote,
in her *Revelations of Divine Love*, that God was 'the ground
of our beseeching' or, to use more contemporary language, 'the foundation of our praying'. He prays with
us and through us. St Paul says something rather similar
in Romans 8:26–7:

> The Spirit too comes to help us in our weakness. For when we
> cannot choose words in order to pray properly, the Spirit himself
> expresses our plea in a way that could never be put into words,
> and God who knows everything in our hearts knows perfectly
> well what he means, and that the pleas of the saints expressed
> by the Spirit are according to the mind of God.

In Matthew 6:8 Jesus reminds us that our Father knows
what we need before we ask him. Therefore God inspires
us to remember those in affliction, for our co-operation
is somehow contributory to his work of spiritual healing.
I firmly believe that God wants every living being to be
fulfilled in its life. It is a difficult dictum when we consider organisms that produce disease, and animals that
may possibly transmit some of them, but here we are in
the realm of mystery, ignorant about the ultimate state
of creation in the love of God. I am sure that it is part

of our work as humans to assist God in this re-creation of the world. Eckhart goes so far as to say that in our world God requires us just as much as we require him.

If this is so, it is entirely the way of God's providence, for he could have worked things otherwise if he had so desired. But the love of God is so great, so immensely caring, that only a fully alive relationship with the one creature on our earth endowed with free will would suffice. And so in intercession God sends his loving care through his human friends to those who are in need of help. The responsibility placed upon the intercessor is enormous, for he or she has made an agreement with God, and that contract cannot be lightly revoked, even during ill health, to say nothing of periods of activity in other spheres. The parable of the Good Samaritan is acutely relevant to the situation, except that the 'neighbour' is truly seen to include everybody.

In my prayer life I intercede by remembering with tender love each individual who comes into my mind from a carefully remembered mental list. I am already 'in God' – in a state of love and dedication – and so my loving contact with the person whom I remember brings, I believe, the full presence of the Holy Spirit to the soul of that person. I believe, in the words of Ephesians 4:25, that we are all parts of one another. Thus I can support anyone through my concern, provided it is sincerely expressed and not neurotically obsessional nor an attempt to prove God by results – 'you must not put the Lord your God to the test,' says St Matthew (4:7, based on Deut. 6:16). Sometimes indeed a remarkable healing may show itself, but this is less important than a change of heart, a *metanoia* in which the mind see things in a fresh perspective.

But how do I remember the person, including many whom I have as yet not met in the flesh? It is soul contact, evoked somehow by the full name of the person. The ancient Hebrews were aware that to know someone's name gave a degree of power over him to the knower;

hence no one could know the name of the Deity in its fullness (Exod. 3:13–15). When I remember the name of someone, whether or not known to me, the love of God 'flows' through me to that person. This 'love of God' I identify with the Holy Spirit, as in the quotation from St Paul's letter to the Romans which I have already mentioned (8:26–7).

I do not spend a great length of time with any one person: it is the contact that is all-important, for on the spiritual, mystical level of reality, time disappears. Sincerity, devotion and faith are the measures of effective prayer, and I have many people to remember. I tend to start with cancer victims, then those whom I have especially served in my capacity as priest, confessor and spiritual healer. Then come the mentally ill, and those in some special need. My brothers in the priesthood play an important part in the great company of those for whom I am instructed to pray; also those who have been of great benefit to me in my own work.

The question arises as to the propriety of remembering some people only amid the great mass of unhealed, suffering victims in the world. I have been instructed that, following the quotation from Ephesians 4:25, sincere prayer for even a few people somehow radiates the power of the intercession to many others. The same principle holds good for the members of religious communities also: remembering a selection spreads the good work to the remainder as well. If one were to intercede for everybody, there would be no time for any other activity.

In the afternoon I likewise intercede for the deceased, mostly in the purgatorial realm, but some probably in a lower region too. This prayer goes on year after year. I have little doubt that at least some of those in the higher ranges of the purgatorial state reciprocate, and their prayers help to strengthen me in this work, which is far from light. Anyone who enters the work of intercession becomes vulnerable to the psychic darkness that surrounds at least some of those prayed for. Indeed, I do deliverance work in the later hours in association with the Evening Office.

My prayer life never ends. When the time of frank intercession finishes, I am still 'in God' as I do my work amongst the various people in my midst, whether in the parish or more privately in the counselling and healing ministry in my own flat, besides the many retreats I am asked to conduct. Of course I fail moment by moment as the 'old man' strives to take over. But the divine presence pulls me up sharply again, without ceremony or fuss, so as to continue this arduous life of service to all those around me.

Prayer – a Creative Activity

Susan Howatch

SUSAN HOWATCH is a bestselling novelist. She has just completed the fifth book (Mystical Paths) *in a series of six about the Church of England.*

As a writer I work all the time with words, so perhaps it is unsurprising that when I pray my inclination is to do without them. However, about three years ago I came to realize that my wordless solitary prayer needed to be complemented by praying in words alongside other people, and that was when I started going to church regularly. I now try to go to church every day. I find the discipline of formal worship provides an increasingly helpful framework as I struggle to become more fully the person God has designed me to be.

I have no doubt that God designed me to write novels and that my job is to write novels exploring the great Christian themes of repentance, forgiveness, redemption, salvation and renewal. Lest this description of my call should sound as if I 'have ideas above my station', let me stress at once that my job is not to be a second Shakespeare or Tolstoy but to be the best possible Susan Howatch – whatever that involves, and from the point of view of literary society it may involve nothing worthy of note. My task is merely to write the books, not to worry about who will read them and how they will be judged; I know I can rely on God to use them in what-ever way he pleases. I am convinced that this is the work God requires of me because it is when I am alone, writing novels, that I feel most fully myself – which means, paradoxically, that I am unaware of myself because I feel completely at one with my Creator.

When I began to read about Christianity after my conversion in 1983 I soon came across the phrase 'To work is to pray' and instantly I knew what that meant, but later I came to view this phrase with suspicion and later still I decided it could be a cop-out. There is indeed a very real sense in which my work is prayer, but because of the solitary nature of the activity I know I have to pray in other ways too in order to avoid the pitfall of self-centredness.

Fortunately prayer, like writing, is a creative activity. I first realized this when I saw on television a series of programmes about prayer given by Dr Una Kroll. Every single one of the processes she described I could parallel in the creative mechanics of writing a novel. Even the cure for 'dryness in prayer' matched the cure for 'writer's block' (i.e. keep at it, no matter how futile it seems, and eventually something will happen). That made me realize that although I was highly skilled at the craft of novel-writing – after forty years' practice, beginning at the age of twelve – I was an absolute beginner at the craft of prayer. On the other hand, the fact that both creative activities had so much in common gave me hope that by hard work and application I might one day be able to pray better.

My prayer usually begins when I sit down to work. I get up early in the morning, and on the wall above my writing-table is a 'Christus Victor' crucifix. I look at it. That means making eye-contact with Jesus Christ – 'the window', as Bishop Robinson put it, 'through which we see God'. Without words I then mentally scoop up the book, or draft, on which I am engaged and offer it to God with thanks for help received in the past and a plea for help in the day to come. After that I touch the keys on my typewriter, flip the switch in my head and tune in. If I am working on the first of my five drafts – creation *ex nihilo* – I would merely pick up my fountain pen instead before pulling the switch. By this means I put myself at one with God and open up the channel which can be used by the creative power of the Holy Spirit to enable me to become most fully myself, playing my own role, no matter how microscopic and unimportant, in God's enormous creation.

When I am not working I still get up early and make eye-contact with my 'Christus Victor', but instead of my work I offer up my brain. This is because I shall be reading and I want God's grace to flow into my mind so that I understand as much as possible. I read theology, church history, biblical criticism, books on liturgy, prayer, mysticism – anything connected with Christianity. I am particularly interested in the interface between Christianity and psychology (explored by my most recent novel, *Mystical Paths*) and the complementarity of science and religion. I read very quickly, but if I like a passage I read it again, slowly, and if I like it very much I stare at it for some time to allow it to resonate in my mind. This would be my version of prayer as *lectio divina*. Although I am a Protestant of the Church of England's 'middle way', I am much attracted to Catholic spirituality in both the Roman and Anglican traditions, and my favourite writers on prayer are Christopher Bryant, Father Andrew SDC and Thomas Merton. I am at present studying Père Grou's essays on the Lord's Prayer.

In the afternoons when I am doing chores, such as shopping at the supermarket, I think about God and open up my mind again in wordless prayer to try to receive any enlightenment he may be sending me about how I can best apply in my everyday life the wisdom which I find in my reading. I am at present theocentric, so these wordless prayers are usually always directed to God, but I have become more aware of Christ since becoming a regular churchgoer.

I have deliberately chosen to live near Westminster Abbey, so I am fortunate enough to have a range of services on offer daily. I usually go to Evensong. This is for me the most balanced of the services, because it not only gives all three members of the Trinity equal billing, but pays due respect to Mary and draws on both the New Testament and the Old. On Sundays I occasionally go to Matins, but at least twice a month I try to attend the Eucharist, which is the service I find most difficult to appreciate. I have never had the slightest desire to take the sacrament, but I have now trained myself to watch without flinching and join in some of the prayers. One has to work at worship, as I was once told severely, and I am working at the Eucharist. To attend is a good discipline for me, but although I have come to see that worship through the eucharistic liturgy is another facet of the creative activity of prayer, it is a facet for which I have no aptitude. When I am present at the Eucharist I feel as a tone-deaf person must feel in the presence of great music.

I always enjoy the beautiful music at the Abbey, but my favourite service of all is Said Evensong when I am distracted neither by the music nor by the movements of the clergy; at the said service the words become like a mantra, invoking a direct awareness of God.

At all the services I like the intercessionary prayers, but best of all are the silences when one can pray for people one knows. I picture the people one by one, wrap them up in my psyche and stroke them. I also like listening to readings from the Bible because the clergy at the Abbey all read wonderfully well and I often hear emphases which have eluded me on the printed page. But the highlight of any Sunday service is the sermon. I love sermons. I pull the switch in my head, open myself up to God and let the words stream through me. Of course sometimes the sermons can be dull and there will be no particular message worth noting, but once I was saved from utter despair by a sermon and I have never forgotten this experience. So whenever a preacher clambers up into the pulpit and mutters: 'In the name of the Father,

Son and Holy Spirit . . .' I feel filled with eager antici-
pation and pray hard that a new moving and meaningful
spiritual insight will be revealed.

As I look back over this chapter I see I have given the
impression that my life is entirely solitary, but in fact the
more I pray the more energy I have to engage with other
people. By aligning me with God, drawing me towards
Christ and making it possible for me to receive more
easily the creative power of the Holy Spirit, prayer has
given me a more balanced, much happier life as I struggle
to serve God as well as I possibly can.

Night and Morning

Sydney Carter

SYDNEY CARTER is a poet whose religious songs are strongly influenced by folk tradition. An Anglican with Catholic and Quaker leanings, he is as unfundamentalist as you can get.

Night and morning now I light a candle before an icon which I have known and loved for years. In it Mary holds the infant Jesus, and he is looking up at her. She, with her arms around him, looks at me. 'Our Father,' I say, 'which art in Heaven.' But by these two I am reminded that the Maker of all things is as much our Mother as our Father; also, that there is a sense in which the Child is the child of all of us. For that which is of God in everyone (as the Quakers put it) must be brought to birth and shown again by what we say and do. 'I once had a dream', writes Meister Eckhart, 'in which I, though a man, was pregnant like a woman with child. I was pregnant with nothingness: out of this nothingness God was born.'

These ideas might have seemed fancy, if not blasphemous, to my father's mother, who first taught me how to pray. A big lady dressed in black, with a silver cross which bounced and dangled on her ample bosom, she told me to kneel down, put my hands together, shut my eyes and say these words:

> Gentle Jesus, meek and mild,
> Look upon a little child,

> Pity my simplicity,
> Suffer me to come to Thee.

I obeyed her, but the last line worried me. Jesus, I understood, lived in Heaven, and that is where you went when
you were dead. I had no wish to go there yet. What
religion was most concerned about, it seemed to me, was
what happened to you after you were dead. Being 'good'
is what you had to be in this world as a kind of insurance
about what might happen in the next, for there was a
place there called 'Hell' which was horrible. If you were
'bad', that is where you went.

My parents rarely went to church but I was sent to
Sunday School. It was there, I think, that I learned the
Lord's Prayer; at the end of which you would say 'God
bless Father and Mother' – and you could also name
anyone else you cared about. I included Felix, our cat,
who used sometimes to sleep under my bedclothes, and
lick me with his rough tongue in the morning. I still
pray, 'Bless Father and Mother', whom I hope to meet
in another place. I add also the names of others I have
loved, or who have loved me, alive or dead.

At the age of eleven-plus my life turned upside down.
I had won a scholarship to Christ's Hospital. This meant
that I would have to leave home and wear a long blue
coat, black breeches and yellow stockings. Dressed like
this, I stood upon the station platform at Christ's Hospital and waved goodbye to my mother and my father.

I was hideously homesick. I felt out of place, with my
north London accent. My father came to visit me to find
out why my letters home were so unhappy. 'Who was
that old tramp I saw you with?' said one boy, 'Was that
your *father*?' For two terms it was like this. Then, one
day, a boy I had hardly noticed sat down by me and
started talking about Jesus. He told me that he and some
others had given their lives to Jesus and invited me to
do the same. I was so amazed that anyone should care
for me to this extent that I adored him on the spot (the

boy, not Jesus) and said 'Yes'. I went to meetings of the Christian Union in an empty classroom, and read a passage of the Bible every day.

As I got more used to school life, and found that I was quite good at rugger, and history, the glory of my 'conversion' faded. I tried to believe that all the Bible said was true, but found it hard. I still enjoyed the hymns we sang in chapel and submitted to confirmation at the hands of Bishop Bell of Chichester; but by now my real place of worship was the school library. History was my chosen subject and the Middle Ages my chosen period: through which I was being led back, through Sabatier's *St Francis of Assisi* and Helen Waddell's *The Wandering Scholars*, to a view of Christian faith very different from the fundamentalist kind which I could not accept. Through a book of Hibbert Lectures on the Reformation I made the acquaintance of the Rhineland mystics and especially of Meister Eckhart. 'Reason is the candle of which faith is the flame,' he said (or something like it). If that's the case, I thought, there's hope for me. The flame is what I longed for, but I could not find the candle. That, I think, is why I began to go to Compline.

There was no shortage of compulsory worship at Christ's Hospital: chapel every morning, and twice on Sunday, with in-house prayers every night. Compline, however, was purely voluntary and wonderfully medieval. St Bernard, St Francis, even Abelard and Héloïse, would have said the very words that we were saying. I loved it, and still do: the darkness, the candles, and the fact that you are not required to recite the Creed, some parts of which I still find difficult. But, 'Into Thy hands, O Lord, I commend my spirit,' I can say at any time: in doubt, in danger, in regret, in grief. If I have a mantra, these nine words could be it.

For many years now, in one notebook or another, I have been copying passages – from the Bible, from newspapers, from novels or whatever – which offer a possible answer, or at least a clue, to those questions which I have been asking and still ask about God, death, pain, sex, ghosts and my duty to my king and country, and to humanity in general. Verses copied from the Bible were mostly those which had come as a shock to me when I had heard them quoted first – like these from Isaiah 45:7:

> I form the light and create darkness;
> I make peace and create evil:
> I the Lord do these things.

Create evil? Surely not. But if God didn't, then who did? Well, Julian of Norwich was puzzled about evil, too. 'If sin had not been, we should all have been clean and like our Lord, as he made us.' So how did sin come about? 'It behoved that there should be sin,' she was told in her vision, 'but all shall be well, and all manner of thing shall be well.' There is much from Julian of Norwich in these notebooks, and from Meister Eckhart too, but St Augustine has been my chief prop from about the age of seventeen, thanks to his *Confessions*.

Into these notebooks I dip, not only as part of my devotions night and morning, but at any time when I need cheering up. Not only that; they take me back to, link me up with, my life as a whole. Why that should help I do not know, but it does. The earliest entry was made on 2 January 1939. I wish now that I had dated every entry, and numbered the pages, so that I could make an index and be able to find particular entries I look for. But in my search I often come across treasures which I had forgotten, like Unamuno's story of Emmanuel the Good, a priest worried by the belief that he was really a fraud: ending with the words of the narrator: 'For I believed then, and I believe now, that God – for I know not what inscrutable purpose – allowed them to believe that they were unbelievers and at the moment of their passing the blindfold was removed.' I had quite forgotten, too, the words of Giordano Bruno, who was burned as a heretic in 1600:

There is only one heaven, an immeasurable domain of light-giving and illuminated bodies; the Godhead is not to be sought far away from us, since we have it in us; so must the inhabitants of other worlds not seek it in ours, since they have it in their own and in themselves.

Laborare est orare (To work is to pray). Can the work of collecting and re-studying these fragments of what saints, heretics and sinners have felt to be the truth be regarded as a form of prayer? I hope so.

There are of course some prayers, or parts of prayers, which have become so much a part of me that I have no need to write them in a notebook. The opening words, for example, of the First Collect in the Anglican Communion Service: 'Almighty God, to whom all hearts be open, all desires known, and from whom no secrets are hid . . .' Thank God for *that*, I always feel!

Select Bibliography

Below is a list of books referred to in the text and some books by contributors:

David Adam, *The Cry of the Deer*, Triangle 1985. (Huggett)

St Augustine, *Confessions*, Penguin Classics 1970. (Carter)

Hans Urs Von Balthasar, *Glory of the Lord*, T. and T. Clark (4 vols.) 1983–1991. (Carey)

Maria Boulding, *Gateway to Hope: An Exploration of Failure*, HarperCollins 1985. (Tilby)

Père J.F. de Caussade, *Self-abandonment to Divine Providence*. (Goodall)

Laurence Freeman, *Light Within*, Darton, Longman and Todd 1986; *The Selfless Self*, Darton, Longman and Todd 1989.

Susan Howatch, *Mystical Paths*, HarperCollins 1992.

Joyce Huggett, *Reaching Out*, Eagle 1992; *Open to God*, Hodder and Stoughton 1989.

Gerard W. Hughes, *God of Surprises*, Darton, Longman and Todd 1985. (Cassidy)

Julian of Norwich, *Revelations of Divine Love*, Penguin Classics 1966. (Israel)

Jurgen Moltmann, *The Spirit of Life*, SCM Press 1992. (Carey)

Paul Sabatier, *St Francis of Assisi*, Hodder and Stoughton 1901. (Carter)

SELECT BIBLIOGRAPHY

Jean Vanier, *I Walk with Jesus*, Editions Pauline 1987. (Huggett)

Helen Waddell, *The Wandering Scholars*, Constable (paperback edn) 1987. (Carter)

The Way of a Pilgrim (ed. R.M. French), Triangle 1986. (Goodall)

Other authors mentioned appreciatively by contributors:

John V. Taylor, Rosemary Haughton, W.H. Vanstone, Alan Ecclestone, Neville Ward. (Cotter)

David Lonsdale. (Campbell-Johnston)

Christopher Bryant, Father Andrew SDC, Thomas Merton, Père Grou. (Howatch)